Serving as the single largest resource ever compiled about Europe's monastery and convent guesthouses, this guidebook features more than four hundred and fifty places of spiritual retreat located in twenty countries. It is an excellent resource for travelers, pil-

grims, summer vacationers, students, armchair travelers, Catholic history or trivia buffs, or anyone interested in monasteries. This handbook provides a key to discovering some of Christianity's most ancient and beloved sites. In these pages you will find all the famous monasteries and abbeys, including those found at Subiaco, Cîteaux, Soligny-la-Trappe, Chartreuse, Monte Cassino, Aylesford, Santo Domingo de Silos, Mt. Athos, and Solesmes.

Inside, you'll find the following invaluable information:

- A thorough history of Christian monasticism
- Complete stories of the major monastic orders
- A chronicle of Gregorian chant
- Contact information for more than 450 monasteries, convents, and places of retreat
- Brief descriptions of each holy place
- Dozens of photographs
- Comprehensive listing of monastic-related Web sites
- Indispensable Internet travel resources

You'll also find many interesting tidbits and fascinating pieces of information from the author, an experienced traveler who has backpacked through eighteen European countries, visiting many of the major shrines, sanctuaries, monasteries, convents, and other places of retreat.

Europe's Monastery

AND

Convent Guesthouses

Europe's Monastery

Monastery

AND

Convent

Guesthouses

◆ *A Pilgrim's Travel Guide* ◆

Kevin J. Wright

Liguori

LIGUORI, MISSOURI

Published by Liguori Publications
Liguori, Missouri
www.liguori.org

Library of Congress Cataloging-in-Publication Data

Wright, Kevin J., 1972–
    Europe's monastery and convent guesthouses : a pilgrim's travel guide / Kevin J. Wright.
        p.   cm.
    Includes bibliographical references and index.
    ISBN 0-7648-0659-9 (pbk.)
    1. Monasteries—Guest accommodations—Europe—Directories. 2. Convents— Guest accommodations—Europe—Directories. 3. Retreats—Europe—Directories. I. Title.

BX2590 .W75 2000
647.94401—dc21   00–040533

Printed in the United States of America
08 07 06 05 04   6 5 4 3 2

*To all monks, hermits, priests, brothers,
nuns, and sisters who have consecrated
their lives to Christ and his Church.*

CONTENTS

Part 4

Other European Places of Retreat

Part 5

Other European Monasteries and Convents

Part 6

Appendices

SPECIAL NOTE

To view maps representing the locations of the monasteries and convents, you can visit the Web site www:catholicadventures.com.

Acknowledgments

WHEN COMPILING a book of this size and magnitude, I find there are so many people to thank. First, I have the incredible pleasure and joy of thanking my dear family friend, Keith Dumm. During our year of working together, Keith provided the spark for the idea to write a guidebook about the monasteries of Europe. After that first spark, he also gave me much encouragement and support, as well as many tips and ideas. Thank you, Keith, for being the inspiration behind this book!

I also have the monumental task of thanking every person from each of the various monasteries, abbeys, convents, and other places of retreat who took the time to correspond with me. However, since it is virtually impossible to adequately thank each of you for your efforts personally, please know that all of you remain close in my prayers. This book is dedicated to you. May God bless you a hundredfold throughout all the days of your life, and thank you for being an image of Christ for us here on earth.

Finally, most particularly to my family and friends, but also to everyone who has supported me while I was writing this book, I would like to offer a special note of gratitude for your encouragement and interest. You were a great support!

And, as always, the ultimate credit, of course, goes to our Blessed Lord and Mother Mary. Without them, I could do nothing. They are the sole reason for writing this book.

Introduction

Europe's Monasteries & Convents: An Angel's Paradise

For many people, the idea of staying in a monastery or convent is attractive. With their mysterious yet peaceful atmospheres, they are not only great sources of spiritual refreshment and renewal, but sacred places of transformation. History is filled with stories of people who traveled great distances just to get a taste of monastic life and experience its fruits.

But the thought of staying overnight at a monastery or convent may be accompanied by a multitude of questions, such as: Is it really possible? Do you have to be Catholic? Can you speak with the monks and nuns? Are you expected to participate in religious services? How does one "make reservations"? Often, the answers to these questions are surprising.

First, *it is possible* to stay overnight at those particular monasteries and convents which are set up to receive guests. Second, one does not have to be Catholic in order to enjoy the fruit of spending a night at one of these places. In fact, there are no faith-related requirements, but one is expected to respect their customs and traditions since you are being "invited into their home."

Third, one of the wonderful aspects of visiting a monastery or convent is that the monks or nuns will often make themselves available to visitors and guests (at appropriate times) for discussions. Having an opportunity to converse with these men and women who have dedicated their lives to Christ can create mutually treasured and insightful moments that last a lifetime.

With regard to the question, "Are you expected to participate in all religious services?" the answer is essentially twofold. Since the purpose behind staying in a monastery or convent is to experience the daily rhythm of their prayer and work life, it should come as no surprise that all guests are strongly encouraged to attend the religious services (for example, Mass, Liturgy of the Hours, and so on). However, since there are certain rituals reserved solely for the practitioners of that particular faith, participation may be dependent upon whatever activity is taking place.

Finally, one may wonder how to go about "making a reservation" at a monastery or convent. Essentially, all one needs to do is contact them, either by letter, phone, fax, or e-mail and express the desire to stay overnight. Even though it may take several attempts, one can usually expect a reply in a reasonable length of time, assuming, of course, that you correspond with them in a language they are able to understand. (For more information about this, please refer to the chapter entitled "Contacting Monasteries, Convents, and Places of Retreat," p. 52.)

In order to help familiarize yourself with some aspects of monasticism, I begin this book with a thorough study of its history. Then, along with an introduction to some popular names and terms associated with monasticism, I provide you with information about how to make the best of your monastic travels. In the next three parts of the book, I list all of the religious places that either offer overnight accommodation, or are wonderful places for day-trip retreats. The book concludes with a comprehensive collection of invaluable Web sites that are related to monasteries and travel.

When setting out to visit these holy sites, it is very important to keep in mind that these places are not to be considered "cheap hotels." Rather, they are living, breathing sanctuaries which foster the spiritual life, not only of their residents (the monks and nuns) but also of their guests as well.

Since many people will use this book to embark on spiritual pilgrimages of their own, I have intentionally designed it to go hand-in-hand with my two previous books: *Catholic Shrines of Western Europe* and *Catholic Shrines of Central & Eastern Europe*. If you would like to learn more about these guidebooks, you can visit my Web site at www.catholicshrines.com.

By writing a book of this nature, I hope to accomplish three things. First, that *Europe's Monastery and Convent Guesthouses* will help facilitate a visit to one of these sacred places. Second, that it will provide a way for all people to learn more about this treasured and ancient tradition of the Catholic Church. Third, that it will serve as an instrument to present monasticism and the religious life to the reader as possible vocations.

With this book, you now have the key to unlock the door to the discovery of some of Christianity's most ancient and beloved sites. Few laypeople ever get the opportunity to have firsthand experience with the daily rhythm of either the monastic or convent life. Now you can make this dream a reality.

SPECIAL NOTE

IN ORDER TO update future editions of this book, please notify me with any changes or additions to the enclosed mailing addresses, telephone/fax numbers, e-mail or Web site addresses. Also, please advise me of any monasteries, convents, or places of retreat which you would like included.

To view maps representing the locations of the monasteries and convents, you can visit the Web site www.catholicadventures.com.

To contact me directly, you can e-mail me at one of the following: • kevin @catholicadventures.com • kevinjwright@juno.com • or write to me c/o my publisher:

Liguori Publications
Attn: Kevin J. Wright, Author
One Liguori Drive • Liguori, MO 63057-9999
Fax: (314) 464-8449

Part 1

✠

Everything You Wanted To Know About Christian Monasticism...But Were Afraid to Ask a Monk

HISTORY OF CHRISTIAN MONASTICISM

FOR THE PAST EIGHTEEN CENTURIES, in various forms, monasticism has existed within the Catholic Church. It is a lifestyle where an individual withdraws from society in order to devote oneself entirely to God through prayer, penance, solitude, and self-denial. Throughout the history of the Church, this devotion has adopted two forms: the anchoritic style, whereby the monk lives by himself or herself as a hermit; and the cenobitic, where the monks live in community. Today, monasticism remains one of the oldest and most treasured traditions of the Church. The faith has profited enormously, both spiritually and intellectually, from this tradition.

Monasticism has existed in the Catholic Church for the past eighteen centuries. Today, it remains one of the oldest and most treasured traditions of the Church.

Although monasticism can be found in other religions throughout history, the origins of Christian monasticism date back to the second half of the third century in Egypt (c. 270). Under the influence of both Clement of Alexandria and Origen, a number of Christians withdrew from society in order to dedicate themselves completely to God and the pursuit of holiness and perfection. Detaching themselves completely from all worldly possessions and relationships, they would spend their days praying, fasting, laboring, studying Scriptures, and performing penitential exercises in order to cleanse both their souls and bodies.

Among these first anchorites, the most famous is Saint Anthony of Egypt (c. 251–356). One of the first to adopt this lifestyle, he attracted a great number of followers through his personal example of living and praying. Today, he is regarded as the Father of Monasticism.

Although the anchorite life blossomed in the Egyptian desert, another form of monasticism soon challenged it. This latter form of monasticism, called cenobitism, would eventually play such a major role that it would create the basis for the formal monastic orders founded in later years. This type of monasticism consisted of a group of like-minded men or women coming together to reside in a community under the authority of an abbot or abbess. Saint Pachomius (d. 346), who organized the first monastic communities in upper Egypt, was primarily responsible for the formulation of the cenobitic lifestyle.

Before long, the monastic idea swiftly swept across Christian lands as many people chose to pursue this path to holiness. Saint Basil the Great, himself, also gave the monastic lifestyle a boost by contributing an extensive theological foundation to it. Furthermore, he fostered the idea that communities such as these should be concerned not only with labor but also with learning. This new way of thinking helped heighten the appeal of monasticism. In time, monasteries soon became important contributors to the intellectual life of the Church.

Although monastic life in the East thrived from earlier on, it took much longer to develop in the West. Loose organizational structures were partly to blame, as many of the monasteries in the West followed the rules of their own individual abbots, thus providing for no uniformity.

However there was one Italian monk who helped put an end to this problem—Saint Benedict of Nursia (d. c. 480–550). As the leader of his own monastery, he wrote and instituted a very useful, yet flexible rule that captured both the guiding principles of earlier monastic customs as well as addressing the practical day-to-day needs of his monks. The excellence of his rule (Rule of Saint Benedict) was such that it spread across the West, facilitating the rise of the Benedictine Order as a major contributor to the civilization of Europe. Also, the impact of his rule was so great that Saint Benedict would earn the title "The Father of Western Monasticism."

Meanwhile, as monasticism continued to spread to other countries, Ireland soon emerged as one of the truly great centers for monastic life since the Irish monks proved to be so numerous and zealous in their approach to the faith, setting out to convert other lands, including Scotland, parts of Germany, Switzerland, and northern Gaul. In fact, many monastic missionaries, not only from Ireland but also from England and modern-day France, set out to bring the faith to Poland, Hungary, Scandinavia, and elsewhere.

During the Carolingian era, the development of the monastic culture steadily continued. Despite the opposition of Saint Benedict of Aniane (d. 821), the Benedictine houses continued to place heavy emphasis upon learning and culture, including the arts (such as manuscript illumination). Throughout the Carolingian Renaissance, many monasteries became important cultural hubs for both education and economic involvement. As a result of their significant contributions to both society and the Church, monasteries gradually acquired wealth, influence, and prestige, while their abbots received royal favors and political rights.

In 910, a much-needed reform of the monastic life began with the founding of Cluny. This event marked the beginning of what was later considered to be the peak of the development of monasticism in the West, lasting from the tenth through the thirteenth centuries. With its call to greater prayer (choir office) and unity among the houses, the Cluniac Reform quickly found widespread appeal. Since many monasteries and abbeys wished to share in the spiritual vigor of Cluny, the abbey soon found itself extending its jurisdiction over more than one thousand houses. Even the Gregorian Reform of the eleventh century, which served to correct moral abuses within the Church, drew much of its inspiration from Cluny.

During this time, monasteries continued to thrive as rich cultural places. Many monks became well-known historians, chroniclers, advisors, theologians, artisans, and architects. While many agreed that the monasteries played a very positive role within society because of their secular contributions, a significant number of monks began clamoring for a return to the religious and spiritual simplicity of earlier times. As a result, new, stricter orders were born including the Carthusians, Camaldolese, Vallambrosians, and Cistercians.

From the thirteenth century on, Western monasticism declined, both in membership and appeal. Although there were many causes, some of the decline was due, in part, to the widespread relaxation of rules and poor leadership exhibited by the abbots. However, one major cause of the decline could also be attributed to the rise of the mendicant orders, which included the Dominicans, Franciscans, and Carmelites. Many potential monks joined these new religious orders of the Church. Although a slight revival of the Benedictine Order took place in the late fourteenth century, it was quickly smothered with the onslaught of the Protestant Reformation.

In many of the lands where the Reformation took root, monasteries were suppressed, ransacked, and looted. Monks were either expelled or executed, while cultural and intellectual treasures were stolen, burned, or destroyed. The worst destruction occurred in Scandinavia and England, where King Henry VIII (1509–1547) plundered and dissolved the communities. Martin Luther, himself an Augustinian monk, added to the chaos through his severe attacks on monasteries in his writing.

As Western monasticism became a quickly sinking ship, a beacon of light eventually emerged when the Catholic Church responded with the Council of Trent (1545–1563) and its own Reformation. Strong decrees of reform, centralization, and revitalization helped not only to save monasticism from obliteration, but to provide it with new energy, vitality, and direction. Among the fruits of this Reformation were the creation of two new monastic congregations: the Maurists (founded in 1621) and the Trappists (founded in 1662).

Although the monasteries would eventually experience a sense of calm, they soon had to once again endure intense struggles as the French Revolution and Napoleonic Wars (1796–1815) almost wiped them off the face of Europe. Because of their destruction, monastic houses throughout France, Switzerland, Germany, and elsewhere virtually vanished overnight.

Fortunately, in the eighteenth century, monasticism began to witness a rebirth as prominent leaders such as Dom Prosper Guéranger (Solesmes, France) oversaw the creation of new houses in France, Belgium, England, America, and Australia. In the nineteenth century, European monastic communities again began to blossom, seeking to open new communities around the world.

Today, monastic orders continue to play a vital role both in the world and the Church. They not only make a great contribution to the intellectual life of society and the Catholic faith, more importantly, they continue to pray unceasingly on behalf of all humankind.

ORDER OF SAINT BENEDICT

RECOGNIZED AS BEING one of the largest and oldest monastic orders in the Church, the Order of Saint Benedict is comprised of both men and women religious who follow the Rule of Saint Benedict. Almost fifteen centuries old, the order was formally established in the sixth century in an effort to continue the highly influential example for monastic life that was set by Saint Benedict of Nursia (c. 480–c. 550).

As Saint Benedict did not actually found an order, the early history of what is referred to as the Benedictine Order was the simple gathering together of various communities under the Benedictine Rule. Although they all operated independently and practiced autonomy, as a whole, they made a great contribution to the development of monasticism throughout Europe. One major supporter of this movement was Pope Saint Gregory I the Great (who was pope from 590–604), himself a Benedictine. In order to help the spread of monasticism and the faith, he sent missionaries to various lands. One of these missionaries was the famed Saint Augustine of Canterbury. Augustine brought the Benedictine rule to England, where it gradually replaced the more austere Rule of Saint Columbanus.

Before long, monasteries began appearing all over Western Europe—in France, England, Spain, Italy, and so on. However, in 817, due to their terrible disorganization, Emperor Louis decreed that some kind of uniformity be implemented, commanding that all monastic communities within the empire adopt the Benedictine Rule. While such a reform proved difficult to enforce owing to the independence practiced by the houses, most of the communities began calling themselves Benedictines.

In the ninth century, further reforms were enacted which attempted a return to greater austerity and asceticism in the monasteries. One of the chief proponents of this cause was Saint Benedict of Aniane (d. 750–821). In the following century, even further reforms took place, primarily due to the Abbey of Cluny. These reforms, particularly those set by Cluny, triggered the rise in the eleventh century of much stricter orders with more centralized monastic governments. Among these new orders were the Carthusians, Cistercians, and Camaldolese. This brought a general revival of monasticism in the West.

The Benedictines, however, remained steadfast in their opposition to institutional centralization, despite the efforts of the Fourth Lateran Council (1215) and the bull Benedictina (1336) of Pope Benedict XII. They did, however, adopt the system of congregations as a means of reform and revitalization. These national and international unions of houses brought improved organization while still permitting their retention of self-determination and identity. Among the most memorable foundations resulting from this was the Congregation of St. Maur (the Maurists), which began in 1621.

However, in subsequent years, monasticism began to witness a decline. Even though this was due to a number of different factors, much of it resulted from the devastation of the Reformation and the Renaissance period. Throughout the medieval era, however, the Benedictines played a major role in the preservation and advancement of learning in Christian Europe, working almost single-handedly to preserve a flicker of culture and civilization in the West during the Dark Ages. For centuries, they were virtually the sole guardians of learning and classical thought.

The Reformation, however, nearly caused the downfall of the Benedictines, as well as many other monastic orders. In England, not only did King Henry VIII (reigned from 1509–1547) ruthlessly suppress the monasteries, he also destroyed and looted many of them. Monasteries in Germany and Scandinavia suffered much the same fate. In the years that followed, the Benedictines again suffered a great deal due to their oppression during the time of the French Revolution and Napoleonic Wars (1796 and 1815).

Fortunately, in the nineteenth century, they witnessed a revival, thanks primarily to a young monk by the name of Dom Prosper Guéranger. Not only did he establish new monasteries throughout France (including the mother house at Solesmes), but he brought a revival of Gregorian chant to the liturgy.

During the past two centuries, the Benedictines have continued to grow throughout the world. In 1846, the first Benedictine house was founded in the United States (Latrobe, Pennsylvania). Today, there are approximately ten thousand Benedictines worldwide who are organized into a number of congregations, including the American, Cassinese, South American, and English Benedictines, as well as the Camaldolese, Sylvestrine, Subiaco, and Olivetan. The Benedictine nuns, founded in 529 by Saint Benedict's sister (Saint Scholastica), are organized into three federations: Saint Scholastica, Saint Gertrude the Great, and Saint Benedict. During the course of their history, the Benedictines have given us twenty-three popes and a number of saints.

CISTERCIAN AND TRAPPIST ORDERS

IN 1098, Saint Robert of Molesmes founded the Cistercian Order. Unlike the Benedictine Order, which received its name based upon its founder, the Cistercian Order was named after its mother house at Cîteaux (in Burgundy, France). The order would retain its Benedictine roots, but institute a much more austere daily program.

Withdrawing from society in order to pursue a life completely dedicated to God, everyday, monks and nuns pray unceasingly on behalf of humankind.

The order came into being, with just a small group of his fellow monks, when Saint Robert became dissatisfied with the lax attitude of his monastery.

Among the first Cistercian abbots were Saint Robert, Saint Alberic, and the famed Saint Stephen Harding. The latter abbot, who served from 1109–1133, is often called the second founder of the Cistercians. In 1119, Harding wrote the constitution of the order, which was subsequently approved by Pope Callistus II. The constitution, called the Charter of Love, called for manual labor, a simplified liturgy, and strict asceticism.

In 1112, during Harding's tenure as abbot, Saint Bernard of Clairvaux, one of the Church's greatest figures, arrived at his doorstep. With his fame and brilliance, he helped to spread the popularity of the order across the continent of Europe.

Cistercian monks adhere to a rigorous life of work and prayer. Although each house could exercise control over its own affairs, it was their duty to strictly adhere to the regulations that were passed by the annual general chapter. This allowed the monks to maintain discipline and introduce new or needed reforms and innovations.

During the 1100s and 1200s, the Cistercians enjoyed widespread prominence, exerting a profound influence on the monasticism of the time. Commonly referred to as the White Monks, they possessed more than five hundred abbeys at the beginning of the thirteenth century, including the famed house of Rievaulx. Unfortunately, the order eventually lost its stature and, like other monastic orders, suffered greatly from the tribulations of the late Middle Ages, Renaissance, and Reformation.

In the 1600s, a reform movement began that called for the return to a more precise adherence to the rule. Known as the Strict Observance, it found support in many of the French houses. This subsequently led, in France, to a division between those practicing the Strict Observance and the others practicing the Common Observance.

During the late seventeenth and early eighteenth centuries, the Cistercians of the Common Observance suffered terribly because of the French Revolution. Fortunately, they did recover and managed to remain intact. With respect to the Cistercians of the Strict Observance, their rallying point centered around the monastery of La Trappe in France during the Revolution. Although the members of La Trappe were expelled at that time, they returned in 1817. With Augustine Lestrange as their new abbot, they revitalized their austere rule and helped to reestablish it in many of their monasteries which had been closed because of the Revolution. As the order began to spread throughout both the country and the world, their members became known as the Trappists, a name that is still popularly used for those of the Strict Observance.

In 1898, the year that Cîteaux was returned to the order, its community chose to join the Strict Observance. Today, the abbot of Cîteaux serves as the general for the Cistercians of the Strict Observance, which still remain a separate body from the Order of Cistercians. Currently, there are more than twenty-five hundred Trappist monks in the world, and approximately fifteen hundred Cistercians (including Cistercian nuns of both the Strict and Common observance). Trappists are distinguished by their white habits and black scapulars.

CARTHUSIAN ORDER

FOUNDED IN 1084 by Saint Bruno, the Carthusians are a contemplative order of monks who adhere to a strict regimen of prayer, self-denial, and solitude. Similar to the Cistercians, the Carthusians took their name from the place of their origin, the La Grande Chartreuse, a valley near Grenoble, France.

Since Saint Bruno never compiled a formal rule for the order during the early years, members were instructed to adhere, in spirit and custom, to the example of the founder. However, over time, this proved to be rather difficult. In 1127, Guigues du Chastel (the fifth prior of La Grande Chartreuse) laid down the first rule. Five years after Guigues wrote the rule, Pope Innocent II approved it. In 1245, the first Carthusian Order of nuns was started.

In 1258, the order issued a new edition of the rule entitled *Statuta Antiqua*, and in 1368, they promulgated another called the *Statuta Nova*. Subsequently, almost one hundred and fifty years later, the order delivered a collection of the various ordinances and a synopsis of the statutes under the title *Tertia Compilatio*. The following year, Johann Amorback printed the rule for the first time, and, in 1581, the *Nova Collectio Statutorum* was published.

Since the time of its foundation, the Carthusian Order has remained one of the strictest and most contemplative orders in the entire Church. Following Saint Bruno's regulations, monks would devote their entire day to silence, prayer, and isolation. With the exception of coming together at morning Mass, Vespers, and for the evening office, they would spend the rest of their time laboring, praying, and eating alone. On certain feast days, however, they would come together to share their meals.

Owing to their almost total removal from society, the Carthusians did not share the unhappy fate that other religious orders experienced during the upheavals of the Middle Ages. Most escaped persecution, but certain members, however, did suffer execution under King Henry VIII in England. The French Revolution, however, was even less kind to the order. As anticlerical legislation swept through France during the 1800s and early 1900s, the Carthusians experienced many misfortunes. In places such as Spain and Italy however, they remained a popular favorite. Today, they can be found throughout the world.

According to a story told by the Carthusians, there was once a pope who felt their Rule was too severe, so he asked the monks to modify it. In response, the Carthusians sent a delegation of twenty-seven monks to Rome to plead their case. When the group arrived at the Vatican, the pontiff found that the youngest member of the group was eighty-eight years old, and the oldest ninety-five. As a result, the Holy Father left the Rule intact.

To this day, the Carthusian Order is considered, by the Church, to be the most perfect model of a penitential and contemplative state.

CAMALDOLESE ORDER

FOUNDED IN 1012, in Italy, by Saint Romuald, the Camaldolese Order is the fruit of one of the strictest monastic reforms of the tenth century. Known by its full title as the Congregation of the Monk Hermits of Camaldoli, the order promotes a very austere form of common life with strict hermetical asceticism. While newer members reside in a stern monastic setting, the more advanced live in the associated hermitage.

Since Saint Romuald never instituted a written rule, in the early years there existed several variations of the Camaldolese life, each differing from the other in organization and type. For example, some monasteries lived more as a community, while others more as hermits. In 1523, this lead to the founding of a reform group called the Congregation of Monte Corona.

Since its beginning, the Camaldolese Order has been revolutionary in its ability to successfully combine aspects of the hermitic life of Eastern monks with the community life of Western monasticism. Even though the monks live and pray alone, they join each other for community prayers. Their daily diets are quite severe: they never eat meat; they abstain from everything except bread and water on Fridays. During Lent, products such as milk, cheese, eggs, and butter are forbidden. Each monk has his own room, workshop, and garden, where he labors alone, yet he still maintains a connection with the other monks for the upkeep of the community.

ORDER OF CLUNY

THE MONASTIC foundation of the Order of Cluny cannot be omitted if we want to fully understand the history of Christian monasticism. It is here, at Cluny, which is located in south-central France, that one of the largest reforms of Western monasticism took place.

First established in 910 by William the Pious, the Cluny Abbey immediately set out to revive the Benedictine Rule. Their first abbot, Berno of Baume (910–927), brought the lives of the monks into greater balance by reducing manual labor and placing a greater emphasis on prayer and worship, especially the choir office.

As the fame and influence of the monastery grew, Cluny's second abbot,

Saint Odo, helped extend the authority of the abbey to other houses while seeking to also change their discipline and organization. In the years that followed, the abbey continued to be blessed with a succession of remarkable leaders since more monasteries throughout France and Italy requested to be placed under their jurisdiction. This dependence not only helped reform many of the monasteries, but it also revitalized them. In fact, Cluny was so successful that it quickly received papal approval to reach out into Spain, Germany, and England. Many members of the order also earned widespread attention for their expertise in religion and other academic matters, serving as advisors and theologians to kings and popes. As one voice, Cluny spoke out against the evils of the time: lay investiture, simony, and clerical lack of self-restraint.

Although Cluny enjoyed unmitigated success for almost three centuries, by the twelfth century, much of its prestige and influence began to wane. This was due, in large part, to the changing social and political climate, but also to the new reforms launched in the Church elsewhere, especially those of the Cistercians. The fact remained, however, they had a great impact on monasticism, as well as on all of Western Christendom. At the height of its glory, Cluny boasted more than a thousand houses, contributing four popes to the Church.

HISTORY OF MENDICANT ORDERS

A HISTORY LESSON about Christian monasticism would not be complete without mentioning the mendicant orders. Who are they? Surprisingly, they include the very priests, brothers, nuns, and sisters which most of us have probably met in our daily lives, including the Franciscans, Dominicans, Carmelites, and Augustinians. Mendicant is a name given to those religious orders who require their members to take a vow of poverty, and to place their trust in God's divine Providence.

Begun in the twelfth century, these orders came about in an effort to combat the widespread vice and materialism of the time, both in the Church and society in general. Individuals who adopted this lifestyle strove to respond to the Church's call for poverty, chastity, obedience, charity, and trust in divine Providence. Among the most prominent figures of the mendicant movement were Saint Francis of Assisi (1181–1226) who founded the Franciscans, and Saint Dominic (1170–1221) who established the Dominicans. Before long, the Carmelites and the Augustinians also joined these two orders by living their evangelical lifestyle.

Although the mendicants initially were the targets of a great deal of opposition from many priests and prelates, their orders quickly grew in popularity among the faithful, especially with the poor. After learning of their cause, the papacy warmly embraced them, giving their enthusiastic support. As well as bringing about considerable reform in the thirteenth century, these mendicant orders produced some of the most outstanding figures in history: Saint Thomas Aquinas, Saint Bonaventure, Saint Teresa of Ávila, Saint John of the Cross, Saint Francis of Assisi, and Saint Dominic.

AUGUSTINIAN CANONS AND HERMITS

ONE OF THE most prominent mendicant orders in the medieval Church was that of the Augustinian Friars. Officially referred to as the Order of the Hermit Friars of Saint Augustine, the order was created from the isolated communities of hermits who strictly adhered to the Rule of Saint Augustine.

In 1256, Pope Alexander IV brought them together, not just for the purpose of organization, but to entrust them with the task of becoming active preachers and religious in society, to follow a more Dominican lifestyle. As a single unit, the order eventually spread throughout Western Europe, evangelizing and preaching. During this time, other less austere congregations joined them.

Martin Luther, himself an Augustinian monk, belonged to the German Reformed Congregation. Although the Hermits were almost completely crushed by the Reformation, they survived intact. Today, they can be found throughout the world. (The more severe Augustinian Recollects were founded in 1588).

There was also another group which belonged to the Augustinian mendicant order called the Canons. Distinct from the Hermits, they were commonly referred to as the "Black Friars," Black Canons, or Regular Canons. They were among the first in the Church to adhere to a common life yet still follow the Rule of Saint Augustine with its call for poverty, celibacy, obedience, and a strict monastic life. It is believed that the Black Friars originated from communities of diocesan priests in Italy and France, some time around the twelfth century.

Although they received sanctions at the Lateran Councils of 1059 and 1063, they subsequently became very popular. By the 1100s, most canons of the Church belonged to the Augustinians, but their prestige began to wane as they found it difficult to reconcile their Rule with the turbulent times of the 1400s and 1500s. Unfortunately, many of their houses were suppressed during the Reformation. In time, however, they recovered and, to this day, some of these congregations continue to exist, including the Premonstratensian Canons and Victorines.

CARMELITES

ALTHOUGH MOST commonly referred to as the Carmelites, this mendicant order's full title is the Order of Our Lady of Mt. Carmel. Founded by Saint Berthold in 1154, they are known to be one of the more contemplative mendicant orders. According to tradition, Saint Berthold first established the community in Palestine, on Mt. Carmel, in the year 1154. Former crusaders, hermits, and pilgrims were said to have made up the group.

In 1209, the Latin patriarch of Jerusalem laid down the first rule for the community. All members were to adhere to a strict regimen of self-mortification, abstinence, and poverty. By the thirteenth century, many of the Carmelites were forced to leave the area because of the downfall of the Crusader States in the Holy Land. In 1247, a majority of them regrouped in England under the influential leadership of Saint Simon Stock. (However, in 1291, all of the Carmelites who had remained in Palestine eventually became martyrs.)

With the election, at the first chapter at Aylesford, Kent, of Saint Simon as prior general of the order, the Carmelites experienced a new wave of vitality and growth. Simon played a very instrumental role in the increase in popularity of the order throughout Europe. He modified the rule to fit life in the West, designed the brown scapular (after a vision of the Blessed Virgin), and encouraged his community members to enter the university. Under his leadership, the Carmelites became a mendicant order which enabled them to spread more quickly throughout all of Christendom. In 1452, the Carmelite nuns, who lived a cloistered life, joined the friars by following the same rule.

By the 1500s, the Carmelite nuns and friars were both in need of a general reform since many of the communities had become too relaxed in their rules and lifestyles. Hence, two prominent figures, Saint Teresa of Ávila (1515–1582) and Saint John of the Cross (1542–1591), initiated reform efforts. Teresa set out to restore the Primitive Rule to the Carmelite cloisters, while still promoting the contemplative life. John of the Cross attempted to accomplish similar reforms within the communities of friars.

However they were met with strong opposition by those members who preferred to keep the less severe Mitigated Rule. In 1593, their resistance led to the division of the Carmelites into two congregations, the Discalced

Carmelites (those who would adhere to the Primitive Rule) and the Calced Carmelites (those who would follow the Mitigated Rule).

As part of their charism, the Carmelites focus most of their effort and activities on prayer, theology, and missionary work. They possess a special love for the Virgin Mary, are dedicated to praying for priests, and wear a brown habit. Recently, they have come back into the spotlight because one of their members, Saint Thérèse of Lisieux, was named a Doctor of the Church. Today, throughout the world, many laypeople belong to the third order of the Carmelites.

DOMINICANS

CORRECTLY REFERRED to as the Order of the Friars Preachers (Ordo Praedicatorum, or O.P.), this mendicant order is more commonly known to us as the Dominicans. Founded in 1216 by Saint Dominic, they were originally established to convert the Albigensian heretics of southern France.

Drawn from all walks of life, the early members of the group traveled throughout the countryside preaching and evangelizing, especially to the Albigensians. In 1215, Dominic received the group's first endorsement from the local bishop, and one year later, received the pope's formal approval and blessing.

In 1217, the order adopted the Augustinian Rule along with some other monastic guidelines. In the years that followed, many of the friars were sent throughout France, Italy, and Spain to preach, attract new candidates, and found new houses. In 1220 and 1221, the Dominicans held two general chapters during which they continued to work out further details about the order's government. During these meetings, they voted to place special emphasis on corporate and individual poverty.

The Dominicans were very innovative in their approach to the contemplative and active life: they accepted many of the principles of monastic life as well as those of the regular clergy. Although they maintained a strong adherence to daily prayer and liturgy, they did not isolate themselves from the world as they would preach to the people daily. This bold new philosophy helped advance the initiatives of the mendicant orders.

Since they did not reside in monasteries, nor spend much of their time doing manual labor, they were often found to be present in or around universities, as they placed much importance on the development of the intellect. In time, they became known for their academic work and were the recipients of high positions within universities. With their keen intellect and strong fidelity to orthodoxy, the Dominican theologians earned the title *Domini Canes* (Watchdogs of the Lord).

As the Dominicans grew in their membership, so did the number of their houses. By the end of the thirteenth century, they had not only expanded to include more than thirteen thousand friars, but could also be found throughout Europe. In that century alone, the Dominicans also produced two of the greatest intellectual giants in the history of the Church: Saint Thomas Aquinas and Saint Albertus Magnus. The Dominicans not only contributed enormously to the intellectual life of the Church, but also to its overall spiritual well being. Like the Franciscan Order, they sent missionaries to Africa, the Middle East, northern Europe, and the Far East.

Unfortunately, after such a glorious century, the Dominicans experienced a period of decline. Since much of this was due to its rule of poverty, it was further complicated, in 1303, by Pope Boniface VIII's command for them to restrict some of their privileges. However, the order received a boost, in 1475, when Pope Sixtus IV rescinded the order's law regarding corporate poverty.

With a new spark and general renewal about discipline and studies, the Dominican Order again began to grow as they opened new houses in Spain and Rome. By doing this, they were able to accelerate the implementation of Saint Thomas Aquinas's teachings under their own gifted Dominican theologians.

Unfortunately, like most of the other religious orders, they suffered major setbacks during the Reformation and the French Revolution. However, unlike other orders, they received the brunt of it. They were singled out both because of their traditional excellence in learning as well as their fierce loyalty to the Holy See. In the nineteenth century, they began to recoup under the leadership of Jean Baptiste Henri Lacordaire.

Today, the Dominican friars number some sixty-five hundred members around the globe. Dominican nuns, founded in 1206 by Saint Dominic, are also found throughout the world today. They are involved in many different apostolic activities, including perpetual adoration, education, hospital work, and the perpetual rosary. Dominicans are most easily recognized by their white habits, which feature a large rosary that hangs from their leather belts. Their habits also include a scapular, white mantle, black cowl, and a black cape.

FRANCISCAN ORDER

EASILY THE most recognizable of the mendicant orders (both in name and appearance), the Franciscan Order was founded by the renowned Saint Francis of Assisi. Although he never originally set out to establish a new religious community, he attracted a number of followers to his way of life simply by his personal example and holiness.

The origins of the Franciscans date back to 1208, the year when its first members joined Saint Francis in his life of poverty, chastity, and prayer. In the following year, when their number grew to twelve, Francis was inspired to travel to Rome to ask Pope Innocent III (reigned from 1198–1216) for his approval. The pope consented, and each of the brothers subsequently took vows of poverty, chastity, and obedience. April 16, 1209, marked the official beginning of the Order of Friars Minor.

With a very strong dedication to poverty, the early Franciscans would travel throughout the region preaching and evangelizing. Before long, a number of women, led by Saint Clare of Assisi, expressed the desire to imitate Francis and his followers. Hence, in 1212, a women's order, named the Poor Ladies (later to be called the Poor Clares, or the Second Order of Saint Francis), was established. Almost ten years later, a group of laypeople wanting to imitate the principles of the Franciscans adopted their own rule. Saint Francis actually wrote the rule himself, but it was then rewritten by Cardinal Ugolino, and eventually approved by Pope Honorius III. These laypeople are commonly referred to as the Third Order of Franciscans.

As the order continued to expand at a rapid rate, further clarification and explanation of the rule was needed. While the "long rule" containing twenty-three chapters was issued in 1221, the pope accepted a shortened version (twelve chapters) in 1223. The rule mandated both corporate and individual poverty, as well as both an active and contemplative life (a rather revolutionary idea for the time).

Since the Church had always strongly encouraged foreign missionary work, Francis made certain that the rule included this aspect of evangelization. It was the first such declaration for any religious order. Serving as an example for others, Francis set out on several missionary trips. Within a few short centuries, the Franciscans would find themselves in such diverse and distant places as China and Africa. During the sixteenth century, the Franciscans would play a major role in the evangelization of the New World.

With the continuing rapid expansion of the order, the Franciscans soon experienced growing pains. Members differed in their opinions about whether the original rule was too severe and impractical. This would become the central crisis facing the order: it was even present before Francis's death in 1226. One of the two differing groups of Friars called themselves the Spirituals; they wanted a precise adherence to the letter of the rule (and the spirit of their saintly founder), but the majority of friars favored a more moderate interpretation. Neither side would temper their position.

In 1310, under the leadership of Saint Bonaventure, who had been superior general of the order from 1257–1274, the Franciscans brought the matter before the Holy See. After many years of discussion and prayer, Pope John XXII decided against the Spirituals. Subsequent to this decision, in 1322, he reversed the rule concerning corporate poverty. Not happy with the decision, many Spirituals left to establish the schismatic body known as the Fraticelli. Within the order, the elimination of the law against personal ownership caused some problems because some members began accumulating wealth, becoming lukewarm in their practice of the rule.

As more reforms were introduced, the internal divisions increased. Eventually, a split occurred among the Franciscans. This was formally recognized in 1415 and accepted by the Council of Constance. The two new groups consisted of the Observants, those who preferred the rules of poverty, and the Conventuals, those who wanted the pope's decision to stay as it was. In 1517, the two groups became permanently separated. The Observants became officially known as the Order of Friars Minor of the Regular Observance, while the Conventuals became known as the Order of Friars Minor Conventual.

In the years that followed, the Observants gave birth to new Franciscan groups including the Capuchins, the Discalced, the Reformati, and the Recollects. The Friars Minor (Observants) continued to thrive during the 1500s, but the French Revolution and Napoleonic Wars provided them with great challenges, as well as destruction. Today, with more than eighteen thousand members, they rank as the second largest religious order in the Church. The Capuchins are listed as the fourth largest with more than eleven thousand members, while the Conventuals number around four thousand members.

Throughout the centuries, the Franciscans and Poor Clares have produced some of the Church's greatest and most famous saints, notably Saint Francis of Assisi, Saint Clare of Assisi, Saint Bonaventure, Saint Anthony of Padua, Saint Bernardine of Siena, Saint Joseph Cupertino, Pope Sixtus IV, Pope Sixtus V, Pope Clement XIV, and countless others.

PREMONSTRATENSIAN CANONS

COMMONLY KNOWN, in the United States, as the Norbertines (and as the White Canons in England), the Premonstratensian Canons were founded in 1120, by Saint Norbert, in Prémontré, France. Combining both a contemplative and active life, the Canons were among the first orders in the history of the Church to successfully carry out both charisms. Hence, it was their order which helped foster the beginning of the mendicant orders in the centuries that followed.

Although Saint Norbert initially adopted the Rule of Saint Augustine, he later adopted many of the Cistercian ways of life, including the practice of rigorous asceticism. One of the major influences on his life was the renowned Saint Bernard of Clairvaux, a personal friend, who served as a Cistercian abbot.

In 1125, Pope Honorius II formally approved the Order of the Premonstratensian Canons. Quickly, it began to spread throughout all of Western Europe. After a short while, the Canons found themselves embarking on missionary campaigns to Eastern Europe, where they gained considerable influence, especially in Hungary.

As time wore on, a number of reforms took place in the order as many of the rules were enforced and practiced to a lesser degree. In fact, several independent congregations arose because of conflicting viewpoints about how the order should be run. Like other orders, the Canons had to pay a heavy price during the French Revolution, watching helplessly as their order almost ceased to exist in the years following the Napoleonic Wars (1796–1815). Fortunately, however, in the past century, the order has once again began to blossom, due mainly to a major revival in Belgium.

Part 2

✠

Standing on Holy Ground

A "WHO'S WHO" IN MONASTICISM

SAINT ANTHONY OF EGYPT (c. 251–356)

Born around 251, today, Saint Anthony of Egypt is recognized as the founder of Christian monasticism. In 269, after giving up all his possessions, he withdrew from society in order to pursue a life of severe asceticism and solitude. Surviving on only bread and water, Anthony spent the next fifteen years praying and meditating while living in a cemetery tomb near his native village. Around 285, he moved to a mountaintop, seeking to gain even greater seclusion and isolation. As word spread about Saint Anthony, more and more people became interested in imitating the hermit's austere lifestyle. Due to his popularity, he left his hermitage in 305 to organize a community of ascetics under a unified rule. Six years later, Anthony left the area to travel to Alexandria where he labored on behalf of the Church, providing moral support to Christian believers who were suffering persecution at the hands of the Roman government. Later, after returning to the desert, he settled on Mount Kolzim (near the Red Sea) with his disciple Macarius where he remained until around 355, when he left to assist Saint Athanasius in defending the Church against the heresy of Arianism. Once this job was finished, he returned, one last time, to Mount Kozim where he remained until the end of his life, providing advice and counsel to his numerous followers. Saint Anthony died in 356, and his feast day is celebrated today throughout the Church on January 17.

SAINT ATHANASIUS (920–1003)

A Byzantine monk, Saint Athanasius is best known for being the founder of the renowned monastic site of Mount Athos. Originally from the Greek Empire of Trebizond, Saint Athanasius founded the monastery of Laura on Mount Athos in 961. It was the first settlement of anchorites on the mountain. Although the hermits who already lived there fiercely opposed him, Athanasius quickly gathered the support of Emperors Nicephorus II Phokas, and John I Tzimiskes. Around 972, the emperors named Athanasius the abbot general of Mount Athos, thus putting him in charge of almost sixty monasteries. Today, he is revered as a major figure in Byzantine monasticism (He is also commonly referred to as *Athanasius the Athonite*). His feast day is July 5.

SAINT BASIL THE GREAT (c. 329–379)

Recognized as one of the greatest doctors of the Church, Saint Basil the Great is honored as one of the eminent Cappadocian Fathers (along with his brother Saint Gregory of Nyssa). After obtaining an excellent education at Caesarea during his youth, Basil underwent a spiritual conversion, in 357, as he embarked on a journey to the monasteries of Egypt, Palestine, and Mesopotamia. Upon his return, he established a monastic community near Annesi. His innovations, and specifically his Rule, later earned him the title "Father of Eastern (or Oriental) Monasticism." In 360, he left his hermitage to take part in the general church council at Constantinople. In the years that followed, he fought unceasingly against the heresies of the day, especially Arianism. On January 1, 379, the great Saint Basil died. Because he was so beloved, his funeral was attended by not only many Christians but also by Jews and non-Christians alike. Today, the Rule of Saint Basil is still followed by the members of the religious life of the Orthodox Churches. Basil is ranked as one of the greatest saints in the Church because of his spiritual achievements and extensive contributions to Christianity during the fourth century. His feast day is January 2.

SAINT BENEDICT OF ANIANE (c. 750–821)

Saint Benedict of Aniane is recognized as being one of the leading monastic reformers in France. Serving under both Pepin II the Short and his son Charlemagne, later, in 773, he became a monk at Saint-Seine. In 779, he established his own monastery at Aniane hoping to reform French monasticism. In 817, the Synod of Aachen granted official approval to his systematization of the Benedictine Rule under the title *Capitulare Monasticum*. In later years, he introduced reforms for all monasteries which subsequently became official policy. His feast day is February 11.

SAINT BENEDICT OF NURSIA (c. 480–c. 550)

Saint Benedict of Nursia, the founder of the monastery of Monte Cassino, is recognized as the Father of Western Monasticism. Born in Nursia and educated at Rome, Saint Benedict left society around 500 in order to pursue a strict ascetic life, and to escape the wickedness and immortality of the world of the day. Settling inside a cave at Subiaco, it was not long before he attracted a number of followers, from the surrounding area, who sought to imitate his lifestyle. However, because of local problems, in 525, Benedict and a few of his brethren left Subiaco for Monte Cassino. After founding a new monastery there, he devoted his efforts to reforming monastic institutions throughout Christendom as well as composing his famous Rule.

Although Benedict never intended to found a religious order, his holy life and the example he set led to the founding of the Benedictines. His influence was far-reaching, as his Rule has had a major impact on both Christianity and Western monasticism. Saint Benedict died around 550, and was buried in Monte Cassino in the same grave as his sister, Saint Scholastica. His feast day is July 11.

SAINT BERNARD OF CLAIRVAUX (1090–1153)

Saint Bernard of Clairvaux is considered to be one of the greatest monastic figures in the medieval Church. Born in France to a noble family, he entered the monastery of Cîteaux at the age of twenty-three and immediately began living a very rigorous and austere life. At Cîteaux, Bernard came under the teaching of the exceptional Abbot, (later Saint) Stephen Harding, who, in 1115, asked him to select a site for a new monastery. After choosing Clairvaux, Pope Callistus II granted its charter, and within a short time, the new monastery gained widespread attention since it had become the center of the Cistercian Order. Saint Bernard quickly earned the respect of many throughout Christendom as a brilliant abbot and mystic. In the years that followed, he preached ceaselessly against the heresies of his day and gathered support for the Second Crusade. Canonized in 1174, Pope Pius VIII named him a Doctor of the Church in 1830. His feast day is August 20.

SAINT BRUNO (c. 1030–1101)

Saint Bruno, along with Saint Robert of Molesmes, was the founder of the Carthusian Order. Born of wealthy parents in Cologne, Germany, Saint Bruno studied at the renowned Cathedral school of Rheims. A brilliant scholar, he served as director of studies at the school for eighteen years, and was later appointed chancellor of his diocese. In the years that followed, Bruno faced many trials because of his many challenges against the corrupt archbishop. Bruno finally returned to Reims, but, despite his popularity, and the expressed wishes of the public that he be named archbishop, he set out with Saint Robert of Molesmes to found a monastic community near Grenoble. Only six years after settling at Chartreuse, Bruno left for Rome, responding to the orders of one of his former students, Pope Urban II. Since the pope needed his counsel, he was not allowed to return to Chartreuse, but was permitted to settle as a hermit at La Torre, Italy, which was near Rome. As a result, La Torre became the second Charterhouse (house of Chartreuse). Saint Bruno remained there until his death in 1101. His feast day is October 6.

SAINT JOHN CASSIAN (365–435)

Saint John Cassian, a monk and ascetic writer, is usually recognized as being the first monk to introduce the Eastern style of monasticism into the West. Although he spent his early days living in Bethlehem, John departed for Egypt where he received eremitical instruction from the Egyptian ascetics in the desert. After a time, in 399, he left for Constantinople, where he studied under the patronage of Saint John Chrysostom. Following his ordination in 405, Saint John Cassian founded the monastery of Saint Victor (at Marseilles, France) and served as its abbot for the remainder of his life. While at Saint Victor (c. 420–429), he wrote two very important works: *Institutes and Conferences*. The *Institutes* (full title: *Institutes of the Monastic Life*) presented the basic rules for the monastic life and was an important source for Saint Benedict in the creation of his own rule; the *Conferences* (full title: *Conferences of the Egyptian Monks or Collations of the Fathers*) presented conversations of the foremost figures of Eastern monasticism, the Fathers of the Desert. Although never canonized a saint in the West, today, he is still venerated as a saint in the Eastern Church. His feast day, however, is celebrated in southern France on July 23.

SAINT COLUMBANUS (c. 543–615)

Saint Columbanus, also known as Saint Columban, is best known for his promotion of monasticism throughout much of Western Europe. Born and educated in Ireland, he left his country around 590 to establish new monasteries on the European continent. Upon reaching Gaul (France), he founded his first two monasteries in the mountains of Vosges. Despite facing many trials and tribulations along the way, he persevered in his quest. Eventually, he was forced to escape to Italy where he founded the monastery of Bobbio (c. 612). By the end of his life, not only had he helped spread monasticism throughout the continent, but he had also instituted a rule for all monasteries to follow. Even though the rule became known for its rigid authority and austerity, it spread quickly throughout France, Germany, and elsewhere in Europe, until it was eventually replaced by the less severe Rule of Saint Benedict. His feast day is November 23.

DOM PROSPER GUÉRANGER (1805–1875)

Dom Prosper Guéranger was a French Benedictine monk who played an extremely important role in reestablishing the Benedictine Order in France, as well as bringing Gregorian chant back to the Church. Ordained in 1827, he purchased the priory of Solesmes in 1833, and worked unceasingly over the next few years to reopen it as a formal Benedictine monastery. In 1837,

Pope Gregory XVI named him the first abbot of Solesmes. As abbot, he became a prominent clergyman in France, working in all of the French dioceses to have the many local variations of the rite replaced by the Roman rite. Among his most famous writings were those about liturgical matters, which included *Liturgical Institutions* (3 vols., 1840–1851) and *The Liturgical Year* (9 vols., 1841–1866).

SAINT MACARIUS (c. a. 300– c. a. 390)

Saint Macarius the Egyptian, also known as Saint Macarius the Great, is credited with being one of the most important Desert Fathers who helped foster monasticism in Christianity. Born in Upper Egypt, he retired, at the age of thirty, to the desert of Scete, seeking a life of solitude. As Macarius's reputation for sanctity, wisdom, and miraculous powers grew, so did the number of his followers. Before long, a colony of hermits was established at the site. It later became a renowned place for monastic pilgrimages. Ordained a priest around 340, Saint Macarius was regarded by writers of his era as being particularly gifted in spiritual leadership and guidance. A strong supporter of Saint Athanasius and very outspoken leader against the heresy of Arianism, Saint Macarius was banished to an island in the Nile in 374. In his later years, he returned to the desert where he spent his final days. His feast day is January 15.

SAINT MARTIN OF TOURS (c. 316–397)

Declared a patron saint of France, Saint Martin of Tours is recognized as being one of the major figures in the evolution and expansion of Western monasticism. The son of a pagan soldier, he was coerced into entering the Roman imperial army at a rather young age. However, after sharing his cloak with a beggar, he was struck with a vision where Christ told him to abandon the military and pursue the spiritual life. Following his request, Saint Martin left the army and, in 360, founded the first monastery in Gaul. Eleven years later, Hilary of Poitiers consecrated him bishop of Tours. Saint Martin never ceased to promote the spread of monasticism, and in time, became known for the numerous conversions that took place within his territory. Revered as a miracle worker during his lifetime, he was one of the earliest non-martyrs to be venerated by the Church. His feast day is November 11.

SAINT ODO OF CLUNY (879–942)

Serving as the second abbot of Cluny, Saint Odo played a major role in the promotion and expansion of the Cluniac monastic reform. Born in Tours, he entered the monastery in 909 as a result of the influence of Saint Berno.

Twenty years later, he became the abbot of Cluny, and eventually played a major role in the reformation of monasteries throughout France, Italy, and the remainder of Christendom. Pope John XI respected Saint Odo greatly, and entrusted further responsibilities of monastic reform to him. His feast day is November 18 (19).

SAINT PACHOMIUS (c. a. 290–c. a. 347)

An Egyptian saint, Saint Pachomius is recognized as the founder of Christian cenobitic (or communal) monasticism. Born near Thebes, Egypt, he converted to Christianity in 313 after serving in the Roman legion. Withdrawing into the desert to seek seclusion, Saint Pachomius served as a disciple under the famed hermit Palemon. A short while later, he founded a community of monks and created a rule for them which called for a balanced life consisting of prayer and work: it was the first such rule in the history of monasticism. Since the rule proved to be so extraordinary and adaptable, Pachomius was able to institute it in all of the ten monasteries he founded, which included both men and women. In the centuries that followed, his rules and teachings exerted great influence on monastic giants such as Saint Basil, Saint Benedict, and Saint John Cassian. Saint Pachomius is venerated by both the Eastern and Western Churches, as well as the Coptic Church. His feast day is May 14.

SAINT PAUL THE HERMIT (d. c. 347)

Saint Paul the Hermit, also known as Paul of Thebes, is traditionally accepted as the first Christian hermit. According to early sources, Saint Paul is said to have escaped to the desert during the Decian persecutions of 249–251. There, he spent the remainder of his life in a cave, passing his days in prayer and penance. The famed Saint Anthony of Egypt visited him on one occasion, seeking instruction about humility. After Paul's death, Anthony buried him in the cloak that had been provided by the great Saint Athanasius. According to legend, two lions were said to have helped dig his grave. His feast day is January 15.

SAINT ROBERT OF MOLESMES (1027–1110)

Saint Robert of Molesmes is honored as one of the founders of the Cistercian Order. Born of noble parents in northeastern France, he entered the Benedictine Order at the age of fifteen. Named an abbot at a very young age, Saint Robert left for Molesmes, in 1075, to help a group of hermits institute the Benedictine Rule. Although the new monastery initially prospered, the hermits soon lost their pious spirit. Saint Robert subsequently left to begin a new hermitage in a nearby forest. When the bishop learned of this, he ordered Robert to return to Molesmes. However, as his efforts for reform again failed, Robert was granted permission, in 1098, to leave the monastery and retire to the forest of Cîteaux. Here, accompanied by six of his monks, he laid the foundations of Cistercian life. However, one year later, responding to the request of the Molesmes monks and a papal legate order, Saint Robert returned to Molesmes. This time, his prayers and leadership succeeded in restoring a true religious spirit to the house. He remained at Molesmes for the remainder of his life. His feast day is April 29.

SAINT ROMUALD (c. 952–1027)

Saint Romuald, the founder of the Camaldolese Order, is best known for instituting one of the strictest monastic reforms in the tenth century. Elected superior of his abbey in 996, Saint Romuald immediately sought to reform the undisciplined life of his monks. After three years, meeting with little success, he left to live in various monasteries and preach the spirit of penance and prayer. Eventually, he assembled a few men who were willing to live the monastic rule of Saint Benedict according to its original requirements. As a gesture of gratitude for land that was donated by the Count Maldolus to build a monastery, Romuald named his new order Camaldolese. The premise of the new order was to blend the eremitic life of Eastern monks with the community life of Western monasticism. Much of the monk's time would be spent in solitude, except when they would join the others for community prayers. Saint Romuald, the founder and abbot, died in his monastery at Val Castro, Italy, in 1027. His feast day is June 19.

SAINT SCHOLASTICA (c. a. 480—c. a. 543)

Saint Scholastica is the natural sister of the famed Saint Benedict of Nursia. Although little is known about her life, she is said to have consecrated herself to God at an early age, moving into a hermitage near her brother at Monte Cassino. According to early records, Saint Scholastica and Saint Benedict would meet once a year at a house close to Monte Cassino to discuss various aspects of their spiritual lives. Three days after their last meeting, she died. Four years after his sister's death, Saint Benedict died and was laid to rest in the same grave. Her feast day is February 10.

SAINT STEPHEN HARDING (d. 1134)

Saint Stephen Harding is considered to be one of the most important English monastic reformers, and is often called the "second founder" of the Cistercians. Born in England, he left his country to study in Paris and Rome.

After joining the monastery of Molesmes, he was sent to become a monk at Cîteaux. Elected abbot in 1109, Stephen insisted that the community continue its strict observance of the rule despite its declining numbers. In 1112, when all seemed hopeless, Saint Bernard of Clairvaux arrived at Cîteaux with thirty monks. This led to a new spirit within the monastery, as the abbey again began to prosper. As a result of an increasing number of monks, new monasteries had to be established. By the time of Saint Stephen's death in 1134, thirteen new houses had been founded under Cîteaux. In 1119, Pope Callistus II approved the *Charter of Love* (the order's constitution), which stipulated the rules covering the government of the monasteries tied to Cîteaux. His feast day is April 17.

LEARNING MONASTIC LINGO

ABBESS

Female equivalent of an abbot; the temporal and spiritual superior elected by a community of nuns, especially in the Benedictine or Cistercian tradition (later extending to the Franciscan Poor Clares and other communities that profess or observe the monastic ideal of stability to a particular place).

ABBEY

A monastery of monks or nuns governed, respectively, by an abbot or abbess who is elected by the community.

ABBOT

Superior of a monastery, a community of monks. By custom, the abbot is elected

Learning some basic monastic history and terms before your travels can enrich your visits to Europe's abbeys and convents a great deal.

for life by the professed members in a ballot that is supposed to be secret. His authority is both quasi-episcopal and paternal; quasi-episcopal because it confers certain territorial jurisdiction, and paternal because he is responsible for the administration of property, maintaining all rules and constitutions, as well as keeping discipline. The title *abbot*, in some orders, has been replaced with the term *prior* (Dominicans), *rector* (Jesuits), or *guardian* (Franciscans).

ABBOT GENERAL

In male monastic orders, such as the Trappists, Carthusians, and Benedictines, which are composed of independent abbeys led by abbots, the abbot general functions as a superior general with limited powers; he may act as a representative of the Order to the Holy See (usually maintaining a residence and office in Rome), and as presider at general chapters of abbots. The powers of the abbot general vary from order to order.

ABBOT, TITULAR

A retired abbot of an active monastery who has been named abbot of a suppressed or defunct monastery.

ACTIVE ORDERS

Those religious institutes in which the members (priests, brothers, or sisters) engage in some form of activity like teaching, nursing, missionary work, and so on. Communities of this type are distinguished from contemplative institutes, those religious institutes in which the monks and nuns remain within their cloisters to chant the Liturgy of the Hours and engage in works for the support of their communities.

ASCETICISM

The rule of life, based on disciplinary practices, such as fasting, vigilance of the tongue, and so on, aimed at controlling desires and repairing for past sins. One accepts this rule as an aid in the realization of Christian perfection. Asceticism enables one to deny oneself earthly pleasures and to strive to follow Jesus perfectly.

AMBROSIAN CHANT

Melodies composed by Saint Ambrose and his followers for use in the Ambrosian Rite of Milan. Although different from the Gregorian chants of the Roman Rite, they played an important role in its evolution.

ANCHORITE

More precisely called either an anchorite (male) or an anchoress (female), a Greek term used to denote a person who withdraws from the world in order to adhere to a life of prayer and humility. The anchorites arose in the early Church as hermitlike individuals who would withdraw from the world and retreat into a private life of solitude. Early anchorite living, however, was never formal, and individuals were free to leave their hermit abode. In later years, the Church established rules to govern their behavior and activities. In early times, the local bishop would enclose anchorites or anchoresses in their cells, where they would be confined forever. The favorite abode for the first anchorites was the Egyptian desert. These individuals became the earliest practitioners of the monastic life which would spread throughout all of Christianity. Carthusians and Camaldolese monks are important examples of practitioners of anchoritic monasticism.

AUGUSTINIAN RULE

In Latin, *Regula Sancti Augustini*, it refers to the rule or body of laws traditionally attributed and thought to have been established by Saint Augustine and, subsequently used by a number of monastic bodies, particularly by the Augustinian Canons. There is considerable debate and discussion among scholars concerning the origins of the rule. It was most likely drawn up during Saint Augustine's lifetime by a devoted disciple and, with his blessing, was used by the communities of men and women in the early fifth century. This remains a source of some debate in scholarly circles. All but forgotten over the succeeding years, it was revived in the eleventh century by the Augustinian Canons and later adapted to the needs of certain orders, such as the Dominicans, Ursulines, and Augustinian Hermits. The rule was, from the sixth century, preserved in two parts: a prologue which established definite monastic observances (the *Regula Secunda*) and a general consideration of the common life (the *Regula ad servos Dei*). In broader terms, the rules call for poverty, obedience, celibacy, and a monastic life.

BAREFOOT FRIARS

The name customarily used for Discalced monks.

BASILIANS

The name given to the members of a number of monastic communities who took their name from Saint Basil the Great and were part of the non-Latin rite of the Catholic Church. Basilians are found in the Byzantine Rite and among the Melkite Catholics.

BASILIAN RULE

A rule of life composed by Saint Basil the Great (329–379), which serves as the basis for monasticism in the Eastern Church. There are two forms, the shorter (consisting of 55 prescriptions) and the longer (consisting of 313). The rule was revised by Saint Theodore the Studite in the eighth century and continues to be used in this latter form. The rule places an emphasis on obedience, with the requirement of manual work and set times for prayer. Opportunity is to be provided for schools for children, and there is to be a provision for caring for the poor.

BIBLE READING

The spiritual exercise of reading the Scriptures as an aid to prayer and meditation. In monastic traditions, this meditative reading is called *Lectio Divina* and is regarded as especially beneficial for the development of a deep interior life. It is recommended that all Christians read from the Bible on a daily basis in order to draw guidance and inspiration from the Word of God.

BLACK FAST

A practice that was formerly observed in the Latin Rite, and is still observed in the Eastern Rite (and in some monastic orders). It denotes a day of penance when only one meal is permitted, in the evening. Meat, dairy products, and alcoholic beverages are forbidden.

BLACK MONKS

Title given to the Benedictine monks during the Middle Ages because of their black religious vestments/habits.

BLACK CANONS

Term used to designate the members of the Augustinian Canons. During the Middle Ages, it was also used to describe the Benedictine monks, although the more common term used for them was Black Monks.

BREVIARY

From Latin meaning abridgement, the term formerly, and still often, used to refer to the book containing the Liturgy of the Hours, or Divine Office. It is called a breviary because the versions prepared for the friars and secular clergy represented an abridgement (shortened version) of the monastic offices.

CALEFACTORY

From Latin meaning to warm: (1) In earlier times, the heated room of a monastery where the monks could warm themselves during breaks in the night offices; (2) At present, in some monastic communities, a term used to designate the recreation room; (3) A hollow globe of glass, silver, or sometimes gold-plated, which was filled with warm water and used, by the priest, to warm his hands during liturgical functions.

CANONICAL HOURS

The sections of the Liturgy of the Hours, or Divine Office, prayed throughout the course of the day, including: Office of Readings (also called Vigils or Matins), Lauds, Prime (now suppressed), Terce, Sext, Nones, Vespers, and Compline.

CANONS REGULAR

The communities of clergy, dating back to the eleventh century who often follow the rule of Saint Augustine, embrace a monastic form of life. The Order of Premonstratensians (Norbertines) is the largest such order which exists today.

CAPPADOCIAN FATHERS

The name given to the three leading fourth-century Christian theologians, Basil the Great, Gregory of Nazianzus, and Gregory of Nyssa. The name was derived from the fact that all three were from Cappadocia.

CELL

From the Latin *cella* meaning a small room describing: (1) The small living quarters allotted to an individual monk, hermit, or other religious; (2) A small group of monks who live apart from their home monastery are said to constitute a cell; (3) In the early Church, a small chapel erected over a tomb.

CELLARER

The title of the monk in an ancient monastery who was responsible for the temporal goods of his community. Today, this monk is called the *procurator*.

CHANT

A type of sacred singing, either recitative in nature, with short two-to-six tones for an accentus, or melodic, in one of three styles: syllabic, neumatic, or melismatic.

CENOBITE

A type of hermit or anchorite who is distinguished by the fact that he or she resides in a community. From the Latin *cenobium*, the cenobites were the precursors of the monastic orders. The Benedictines and Cistercians are considered cenobitic.

CLOISTER

From the Latin *claustrum* meaning bar or bolt, and from *claudere* meaning to close, it is the term used to describe a limited access to particular monastic communities who willingly embrace the contemplative life and thereby separate themselves from life in the world. A cloistered religious has limited opportunities to leave his or her cloister. Similarly, outsiders are restricted from entering the cloister. Cloistered monasteries are frequently surrounded by high walls to preserve the privacy of the enclosure and to keep the outside world at a distance. Cloister can also refer to this physical enclosure itself. In architecture, the term cloister is often restricted to describe the covered passageway around the open courtyard or quadrangle, which is technically called the garth, located at the center of an enclosed monastery.

CLUNY

Founded in 910, this Benedictine abbey, named after the south-central French village where it was built, was the center of spiritual renewal. It was distinguished by profound prayer and adherence to the Rule of Saint Benedict. Religious houses similar to Cluny sprang up in England, Germany, Italy, and Spain. The influence of this abbey, which existed until 1790, waned in the twelfth century.

COENOBIUM (ALSO COENOBITES)

Derived from the Greek *koinon* meaning common, coenobium is the ecclesiastical term used to refer to a group of monks who live their religious lives in community. The individual in this community is called a coenobite or cenobite, a term that was used in the early Church to refer to monks. While Isidore of Seville reflects a knowledge of the Greek etymology, he also relates this term to the Latin *cena* (meal), since the coenobites, in contrast to the hermits and anchorites, would share their meals in community. Saint Pachomius (c. a. 290–347), author of the earliest rule for coenobites, is honored as the "Founder of Monasticism." Coenobium is also the Latin name for the monastery where the coenobites lived their community life; it can also be the specific name for the monastery church, to distinguish it from the other buildings.

CONTEMPLATIVE ORDERS

Those religious orders in which the monks and nuns remain within their cloisters to chant the Liturgy of the Hours and engage in works for the support of their communities. To be distinguished from the active orders.

CONVENT

The building, or group of buildings, where a religious community lives.

COWL

A term used to describe either (1) hood worn by monks and other religious; or (2) long-hooded robe worn by monastic men and women during the chanting of the Office.

DAY HOURS

In liturgical usage, the word "Hour" refers to any section of the daily cycle of prayer, known in its totality, officially since Vatican II, as "the Liturgy of the Hours," and formerly referred to as "the Divine Office." Technically, the term "day hours" is best suited to what is now called Daytime Prayer, which may (but need not) be celebrated in three sections: midmorning (officially, Terce, or the "third" hour, about 9:00 A.M.); midday (Sext, the "sixth" hour, at noon); and midafternoon (None, the "ninth" hour, about 3:00 P.M.). Only one of these "Hours" is obligatory for priests and religious working in an active apostolate. Contemplatives are expected to keep the traditional sequence.

DISSOLUTION OF THE MONASTERIES

The harsh and often brutal liquidation of the monasteries of England under King Henry VIII (reigned from 1509–1547), a particularly dark episode in the English Reformation. While the monasteries of England had been targets of complaints in the late Middle Ages due to their laxity and corruption, no extensive programs of reform had been introduced. As a result, by the Tudor era, a small number had become quite infamous for their abuses and a few were suppressed. No action on a grand scale was contemplated either during the reign of Henry VII (from 1485–1509) or in the early part of that of Henry VIII. This situation changed, however, as a result of two circumstances: Henry's desire to advance his claims of supremacy over the Church of England, and his dire need for money to bolster his depleted treasury. The monasteries, generally staunch supporters of the papacy, and often very wealthy because of their treasures and gifts, proved to be a tempting target. With the help of his able, but unscrupulous minister, Thomas Cromwell, Henry secured a report that, not surprisingly, found the monasteries to be hives of corruption. In fact, only a tiny number of houses were actually visited and abuses were minimal. Based upon this false report, the Act for the Dissolution of Smaller Monasteries was passed in 1536, putting an end to those houses who had an annual value below

£250. In October 1536, an uprising, called the Pilgrimage of Grace, arose to protest this measure which was swiftly put down. Having seized the goods of some two hundred fifty monasteries, in 1539, Henry and his agents passed the Act for the Dissolution of Greater Monasteries. In early 1540, the last houses had been suppressed and the treasury was considerably enhanced. The dissolution had caused the displacement of a large number of clergy. Most of the priests were either pensioned or compelled to enter the ranks of the clergy of the Church of England. Nuns spent years in disrepute and received pitiful pensions. The monks, who had been the focus of Henry's program, were the most harshly treated. As well as this tragedy, there was the catastrophic loss of valuable manuscripts, works of art, treasures, and buildings which were either seized, looted, or destroyed by Henry's officials. Moreover, England lost an educational tradition that dated back over a millennium.

DIVINE OFFICE

The former name for the official, public (although often recited privately), daily liturgical prayer by which the Church sanctifies the hours of the day. The Vatican II revision of this prayer is entitled the *Liturgy of the Hours*, although the title page of the official books still bears the designation "*The Divine Office: revised by decree of the Second Vatican Ecumenical Council.*" *Officium* was the common Latin word referring to public services of prayer, and indeed "office" is still more or less commonly used among the Churches of the Reformation to describe their non-Eucharistic worship services.

DOM

A title used before the names of monks of certain monasteries, mainly the Benedictines and Carthusians.

EASTERN MONASTICISM

Christian monasticism originated in the East in early third-century Egypt when Saint Anthony (A.D. 251–356) sold all his possessions and went into the desert to more perfectly follow Christ. When he attracted followers, he organized them into a community of hermits under a rule (later formulated as the Rule of Saint Pachomius). The Eastern models were imitated by Saint John Cassian and Saint Martin of Tours in the West. While Western monasticism eventually came to be shaped by Saint Benedict's adaptation of Eastern models, in the East, it was the Rule of Saint Basil the Great (mid-fourth century) that had the widest influence. Eastern monasticism evolved into two principal forms: cenobitic (large communities living under one roof) and idiorhythmic (groups of individuals living in separate quarters and coming together for meals and prayer). Monasticism flourished in the Byzantine world, spreading from Greece to Russia and the Slavic countries. Despite persecution, monasticism remained a powerful force throughout the Communist period, and has now emerged as an important source of Christian renewal in Eastern Europe.

FAMILIAR

A layperson who lives and works within a monastic community but who has taken no religious vows. Such a person has a share in the spiritual benefits of the prayers and good works of the religious community with which he lives.

FRIAR

From the Latin *frater*, French *frère*, Middle English *fryer* all meaning brother. The term is used to describe a member of one of the mendicant orders. The term distinguishes the mendicant's itinerant apostolic character, exercised broadly under the jurisdiction of a superior general, from the older monastic orders' allegiance to a single monastery, formalized by their vow of stability. The most significant orders of friars are the Dominicans, Franciscans, Carmelites, and Augustinians.

GRADUALE ROMANUM

It is the liturgical book containing Gregorian chant notation and Latin text of the proper chants sung at Mass (that is, introit, responsorial psalm, alleluia, and so on). It is to be distinguished from the *Liber Usualis*, which contains all the chants for Mass plus the musical notations and texts for much of the Divine Office. The post-conciliar *Graduale Romanum* is an adaptation of its predecessor in accordance with the directives of *Sacrosanctum Concilium*, the Constitution on the Sacred Liturgy. It eliminates Mass propers that are no longer in common use (for example, the season of Septuagesima, octave of Pentecost), transfers the texts of those saints whose feast days have been changed, and adds new chants for new Mass propers. A shortened version, "for use in smaller churches," has been published in accordance with *Sacrosanctum Concilium* under the title *Graduale Simplex*.

GREGORIAN CHANT

A plain chant with more individuality and characteristic expression than other early chants (such as Ambrosian). These chants appear to have been compiled and arranged by Pope Saint Gregory the Great (540–604), hence the name "Gregorian." After Vatican II and the introduction of the vernacular into the liturgy, Gregorian chant was put aside by most Church musicians. In 1974, however, a publication entitled *"Letter to Bishops on the Minimum Repertoire of Plain Chant"* was sent to all bishops and heads of religious congregations throughout the world. This letter spoke of *Jubilate Deo*, which contains basic chants that should be taught to all, a copy of which was also included.

GREGORIAN MODES

The eight musical scales used in Gregorian chant, divided into authentic and plagal groups. Only one accidental occurs in the Gregorian modes, the half-tone lowering of the seventh note of the scale to "B flat."

GYROVAGI

The term refers to wandering monks who are either not attached to a monastic community or never reside in their proper community. This has always been regarded by Church authorities as an abuse.

HERMIT

From the Greek word *eremites*, meaning one who dwells in the desert, it refers to a religious ascetic who lives a solitary life for purpose of the contemplation of God through silence, penance, and prayer. The hermits first arose in the Church in the third century. The eremetical life was to exercise a profound influence on the rise of monasticism. The Christian era foundation/basis for the hermit is traced back to Elijah in the Old Testament and Saint John the Baptist in the New Testament.

HIEROMONK

A monk invested with the priesthood in the Eastern Church.

HOOD

A conical, flexible, brimless headdress that, when worn, covers the entire head but not the face. It is either a separate garment or part of a cloak. Today, the hood is usually associated with orders that are comprised of contemplatives, monks as well as nuns and/or mendicants.

HOURS, LITTLE

The four lesser sections of the Divine Office that took their names from the times of the day when they were recited. Originally prime, terce, sext, and none, they have been replaced by one "hour" called daytime prayer in the revised *Liturgy of the Hours*.

LIBER USUALIS

It is a book of Gregorian chants for the Ordinary and Propers of Masses, chants for rites and special Masses, and chants of the Divine Office. Edited by the Benedictine monks of Solesmes, the chants of the Liber are of great historical value and, while the book is currently out of print, today it can still be used at Mass.

LITTLE OFFICE OF THE BLESSED VIRGIN MARY

A devotion to Our Lady consisting of hymns, antiphons, psalms, and collects arranged according to a single day's cycle of "canonical hours" based on the model of the Divine Office. Since the advent of the new *Liturgy of the Hours*, the Little Office of the Blessed Virgin Mary has been preserved, almost in its entirety, through the use of a Saturday memorial of the B.V.M. during Ordinary Time. A new and somewhat expanded edition of the Little Office was published as recently as 1986 in England and 1988 in the United States. This edition suffices for those who are not required to pray the Liturgy of the Hours or those who may find the book too expensive to purchase, or too daunting to use.

LITURGY OF THE HOURS

The official cycle of the Church's daily prayer. It was formerly called the Divine Office (a title still frequently used). The renewal of the Liturgy of the Hours at Vatican II called for the public celebration of the Hours whenever possible. Whether recited privately or publicly, the Liturgy of the Hours has the following structure: Morning Prayer (Lauds), Midday Prayer (Terce, Sext, or None), Evening Prayer (Vespers), Night Prayer (Compline), and the Office of Readings. The First Hour (Prime), while suppressed for the universal Church, continues to be observed in contemplative monastic communities. There is an obligation to pray at least one of the Midday Hours, but Contemplative communities should, however, recite all of them. The Liturgy of the Hours consists of hymns, antiphons, psalms, selections from sacred Scripture, readings from the Church Fathers, commentaries on the Scriptures and Christian life, writings of the saints, and standard Catholic prayers. It is arranged according to a four-week cycle called a Psalter. Normally, the Liturgy of the Hours is available in a four-volume set (it is three volumes in England and Ireland). There is also a one-volume abbreviated edition available.

MANDYAS

This terms refers to the monk's full-length vesture in the Byzantine Church, which differs in color and symbolism from the lower clergy's simple black cloak, and the ornate vestments of the archimandrite and the bishop.

MATINS

It is from the Latin term *tempora matutina* meaning morning hours. Originally called the morning hours of Lauds (Laudes matutinae). Later, it referred to the preceding hour of Vigils, sung around midnight. These vigils were eventually incorporated into monastic practice and evolved into the hour of the Divine Office known as Matins. Matins has the following structure: Psalm 95(94) (the invitatory); hymn; Psalms; readings from sacred Scripture; commentaries on sacred Scripture (or, on feast days, an appropriate reading); Responsories; Canticle on solemn feasts.

MAURISTS

Members of the French Congregation of Benedictines (O.S.B.), founded by Saint Maur in 1618, but dissolved as a consequence of the anticlericalism of the French Revolution. Maurists are mainly associated with hagiography because of their research into the lives of the saints. Their work survived the demise of their order through the continued publication of the *Acta Sanctorum*. From their ranks came Montfaucon and Mabillon, the founders of Greek and Latin paleography.

MONASTERY

The house of a religious community, usually, in current usage, the cloistered or contemplative type. The typical monastery is constructed around a quadrangle (the cloister garth), containing a church or chapel, a refectory, chapter hall, common room, work rooms, and individual rooms (cells) for the residents (monks or nuns). The entire physical property of the monastery, or at least some portion of it, is called the enclosure and is normally closed to the public.

MONASTICISM

The lifestyle followed by those persons who choose to withdraw from society in order to devote themselves totally to God through prayer, penance, and solitude. Two types of monasticisms have emerged: anchoritic (where the monks or nuns live as hermits and come together for prayer and certain meals); and cenobitic (where they live in community). Saint Anthony is regarded as the Father of Monasticism, but another monk, Saint Pachomius, formulated the first monastic rule. In Eastern Christianity, the most influential monastic rule is that of Saint Basil, while in the West, the Rules of Saint Benedict and Saint Augustine have prevailed. In both the East and West, monasticism has proved to be a highly durable form of Christian life. It has contributed enormously to the vitality of the Church and the wider culture. Important examples of anchoritic monasticism in the West include the Carthusians and Camaldolese, while Benedictines and Cistericians are representative of the cenobitic type.

MONK

From Greek word *monachos* meaning one who lives alone, it refers to a person who withdraws from society in order to pursue a life totally dedicated to God in prayer, penance, and solitude. Monks are commonly distinguished from communities of clerics or friars who engage in some form of active ministry. While the term "monk" can refer both to men and women monastic religious, common English usage restricts it to men and prefers the term "nun" for women.

NOCTURN

From Latin word *nocturnus* meaning of the night, it originally referred the whole of the night office (Matins and Lauds). Later, it came to refer to just a part of Matins (three nocturns on feasts, one nocturn on ferias). For monks, two nocturns were usual practice (up to twelve psalms and readings for Matins).

NUN

In the strictest sense, the term refers to a woman who belongs to a religious order with solemn vows, but it is commonly used to refer to any woman religious.

OBLATE

From the Latin word *oblatus* meaning offered, it originally referred to those children who were sent to a monastery with the intention of remaining there to study and be raised by the monks. In modern use, it can refer to a layperson who is united to a religious order by simple vows.

OFFICE

Properly called the Divine Office, it refers to the official daily prayers of the Church. The Office is now called the *Liturgy of the Hours*. It can also refer to any portion of the Divine Office that might be recited.

OFFICE OF THE DEAD

The portion of the *Liturgy of the Hours* that is chanted or recited for the happy repose of the deceased. It is prayed on All Souls' Day and may be used after a death.

PLAINCHANT

A term that is originally from the Latin words *planus* meaning flat or level and *cantus* meaning song. It is also referred to as plainsong, an ancient monodic chant consisting of an unaccompanied melodic line, usually sung with Latin text, that is used within the liturgy of the Church.

PRIME

Literally "first," from the Latin title of this part of the Divine Office, *ad primam*, meaning at the first hour of the day. Prime began in monastic communities as an additional prayer before the morning work period. Prime consisted of the reading of the martyrology (or saint of the day), a selection from the monastic Rule and a prayer to "prosper from the work of our hands." In the reform of the Divine Office following Vatican II, Prime was suppressed and the obligation to pray it was removed. However, some monastic communities continue to use the Office of Prime because the *Psalterium Monasticum* (Monastic Psalter) makes allowances for its celebration.

PRIORY

The house of a monastic order that is governed by a prior or prioress. Some priories are "conventual" (that is, autonomous but not an abbey), "simple" or "obedientiary" (that is, dependencies of abbeys).

PRIOR

The title for the leader of certain male monastic communities. The prior can also be the assistant to an abbot.

PRIORESS

The woman religious superior who governs her community, much as a prior is superior over friars or monks.

RULE

The basic regulations of a religious institute, encompassing its daily order and discipline.

RULE OF SAINT BENEDICT

A monastic rule drawn up by Saint Benedict of Nursia (c. 480–547) as the basis for uniting the practices of a community of monks who gathered around him. Saint Benedict consulted other monastic rules in order to develop his own. The Rule is distinguished by its common sense, balance, an emphasis on following Christ, chanting the Divine Office, stability, work, and the leadership of an elected abbot. The Rule of Saint Benedict has been the most influential and widely used monastic rule in the West.

SEXT

That part of the Divine Office which is said at midday.

SISTER

In popular use, it refers to any woman religious; in strict terms, the title applies only to women belonging to institutes whose members never professed solemn vows. Most of the institutes whose members are properly called Sisters were established either during or since the nineteenth century. Women who take solemn vows, or belong to institutes whose members formerly profess solemn vows, are properly called nuns.

SOLESMES

The French village that is home to the Benedictine Abbey known for its monks' work in restoring Gregorian chant melodies to their original form. Their famed abbot, Prosper Guéranger, was responsible for coordinating the publishing of the *Liber Usualis*.

THE GREAT CHARTREUSE

Established in 1084 by Saint Bruno, the Great Charterhouse is the name of the original foundation house of the Carthusian monks. The popular liqueur called Chartreuse originated at The Great Charterhouse and was made by the monks.

TONES

In the Eastern churches, a method of eight standard melodies with variations for plain chant.

TONSURE

The custom of shaving part (or all) of the hair on the head, originating with monastic observance in the fourth and fifth centuries. This custom was retained until the reform of minor orders after the Second Vatican Council. When it was in use, tonsure symbolized admission to the clerical state.

VOTIVE OFFICE

Similar to votive Masses because these can substitute for the regular daily office on particular occasions. The General Instruction of the Liturgy of the Hours states that "for a public cause or out of devotion [except on solemnities and certain feasts]...a votive office may be celebrated, in whole or in part: that is, on the occasion of a pilgrimage, a local feast, or the external solemnity of a saint." The clearest example in the present edition of the *Liturgy of the Hours* is the Office for the Dead.

GREGORIAN CHANT: MUSIC OF THE ANGELS

WHEN ONE thinks of monasteries, the sounds of Gregorian chant often come to mind. Although this form of music is heard less and less in the churches of today, its popularity, nevertheless, continues to grow at an accelerating rate. One example of this may be the fact that the recordings of Gregorian chant by the monks of Santo Domingo de Silos "hit number one" on the European pop charts and made a major splash in the United States in the mid 1990s.

What exactly is Gregorian chant? It is the name given to the form of plain chant that was traditionally believed to have been organized and arranged by Pope Saint Gregory I in the fifth and sixth centuries (hence, the name *Gregorian chant*). Believed to have originated from Jewish sources, the chant is a vocal form of music which uses a conventional scale of eight notes. Since the time of Pope Gregory, the chant has continued to evolve and change, mostly due to its adaptation to different regions. Unfortunately however, by the eleventh century, since the music had become increasingly very complex and ornate, it could only be mastered by extensively trained choirs. As a result, general interest and appeal in chant began a steady decline in the years that followed, in spite of the small revival it enjoyed after the Council of Trent (1545–1563).

In the 1800s, however, the Benedictine Abbey of Solesmes sparked a renewed appreciation for this form of music. Then, in the twentieth century, many of the popes, including Pope Saint Pius X (reigned 1903–1914), Pope Pius XI (reigned 1922–1939) and Pope Pius XII (reigned 1939–1958), helped further the cause of Gregorian chant. The Second Vatican Council strongly promoted Gregorian chant through its document *Sacrosanctum Concilium* (Constitution on the Sacred Liturgy), which stated that this form of sacred music was to "be given pride of place in liturgical services."

However, in the past forty years, despite calls for its continued application, Gregorian chant has essentially been relegated to the monasteries. Ironically, in recent years, Gregorian chant has enjoyed a renaissance in secular music. Many professional choirs and schola cantorums have taken up this music with vigor. Fortunately, with the advent of CDs and cassette tapes, today it is possible to bring the ancient sounds of the monks into one's own home.

GREGORIAN CHANT WEB SITE(S)

There are literally hundreds of excellent Gregorian chant Web sites on the Internet which feature everything from chant resources to choirs to recordings to publications. My best advice is to visit the Benedictine Abbey of Solesmes Web site (see story below) at www.solesmes.com. From their home page, click on the button "Our Links," then click on "Web sites on Gregorian chant." Then, by clicking again on the various options listed (for example, Gregorian Schola), you will have access to hundreds of Gregorian chant Web sites.

RESOURCES

An Overview of Gregorian Chant by Dom Jacques Hourlier (Paraclete Press, 1996); *Reflections on the Spirituality of Gregorian Chant* by Dom Eugène Cardine (Paraclete Press, 1995).

Our Sunday Visitor's Catholic Encyclopedia & Catholic Dictionary. Huntington, Indiana: Our Sunday Visitor, 1994.

Our Sunday Visitor's Catholic History & Catholic Dictionary. Huntington, Indiana: Our Sunday Visitor, 1995.

Welcome to the Catholic Church on CD-Rom. Gervais, Oregon: Harmony Media, 1996.

BENEDICTINE CONGREGATION OF SOLESMES

IN THE PAST two centuries, no other branch of the Church has made an impact on monasticism as much as the Benedictine Congregation of Solesmes. Since the early 1800s, they have served as leaders in the liturgical renewal and restoration of Gregorian chant, while at the same time, also influencing and founding nu-

In the past two centuries, no other monastic branch of the Church has made an impact on monasticism as much as the Benedictine Congregation of Solesmes. Today, they are likened to the legendary monastery of Cluny during the Middle Ages.

merous other monasteries throughout Europe, as well as other parts of the world. Likened to the legendary monastery of Cluny during the Middle Ages, the congregation of Solesmes owes its prominence principally to one man, and to one abbey—Dom Guéranger and the Abbey of Saint Peter.

Located in the countryside of western France, the Abbey of Saint Peter (along with the women's Abbey of Cecilia) today flourishes as a worldwide center of Gregorian chant spirituality and performance. Approximately eighty monks belong to the Solesmes community of men, and about sixty nuns to the Solesmes community of women. Both have achieved worldwide recognition for their contributions to restoring the true Gregorian chant of the Church.

For more than a century, the Benedictine monks and nuns of Solesmes have been heavily involved in the research of Gregorian chant. One of their aims is to assimilate the spiritual riches it contains into the life of prayer within the Church. Many people throughout the world are familiar with the Benedictine monks of Solesmes through their recordings and publications. As well as chant, the monks do extensive research and writing about monastic traditions and papal teachings.

The men's monastery was founded at Solesmes in 1010, but it was closed during the devastating time of the French Revolution. In 1833, a young priest from the local diocese, Father Guéranger, purchased the deserted building. Within five years, he had not only received the Vatican's recognition for his newly established Benedictine community but also had the status of his priory raised to the dignity of an abbey. Furthermore, the abbey would serve as the head of the newly established Congregation of Solesmes, the successor to the Congregations of Saint Maurus and Saint Vanne, as well as the more venerable and ancient family monasteries belonging to Cluny.

Initiating a rediscovery of Christian tradition, the soon-to-be first abbot of Solesmes extensively researched Church history, liturgy, Gregorian chant, and holy Scripture. Wanting to reinstate it as "a center for prayer and studies in service to the Church," Dom Guéranger underscored both the primacy of the Divine Office and the liturgy with his monks, as well as the pursuit of the intellectual life. He knew that a persistent search for the truth was a prerequisite for an authentic spiritual life for monks.

In his most famous work, *The Liturgical Year*, Dom Guéranger not only taught his monks but also the entire world to live by and in the Church, and to pray with her and as she does. Believing the Church's chant to be the most perfect expression of her liturgical prayer, with his monks, he undertook the task of the restoration of Gregorian (chant) melodies which centuries of neglect and change had left virtually unrecognizable. After his death in 1875, the monks continued his work, and today they remain in the forefront of papal, monastic, and Gregorian chant research.

In 1866, with the help of Mother Cecilia Bruyère, Dom Guéranger also founded the women's monastery of Saint Cecilia in 1866. In large part due to the growth of Solesmes, several other monasteries were also either revived or established under his jurisdiction. In the years following his death, the monks of Solesmes founded more than two dozen abbeys and houses. Among these are the renowned monasteries of Fontgambault, Clervaux, Liguge, Saint-Wandrille, Wisques, Ganagobie, and Santo Domingo de Silos (the home of the world-famous monks whose recordings of Gregorian chant "hit number one" on the European pop charts in the mid 1990s). In 1981, they opened their first monastery in the United States, a women's abbey in Westfield, Vermont. To this day, they continue to expand; in the last two years, Solesmes has founded the priory of Palendriai in Lithuania, and Fontgombault, a daughter-house, has founded the priory in Clear Creek, Oklahoma.

What distinguishes the Solesmes Congregation from all others in the Benedictine Order is that all the monasteries are wholly contemplative, foregoing any pastoral or outside responsibilities. Their vocation is truly the splendor with which they celebrate the liturgy of the Church. Every day, they spend four or more hours in community prayer, one hour in personal prayer, and the remainder of their time is spent in doing manual labor, studying, or in recreation. At the heart of each abbey's community life are the Mass and the Liturgy of the Hours.

In accordance with Vatican II and the Constitution on the Sacred Liturgy, the monks and nuns of Solesmes have "preserved the use of the Latin language and given prominent place to Gregorian chant" in their liturgies. They also give special attention to the visual aspects of the Mass with their vestments, ceremonial practices, and incense. The result is Solesmes's world-renowned role in the liturgical renewal and restoration of Gregorian chant today.

SOLESMES WEB SITE

To learn more about the Benedictine Congregation of Solesmes, visit their Web site at: www.solesmes.com.

CONTACT INFORMATION

Abbaye Saint-Pierre
1 Place Dom Guéranger
72300 Solesmes (France)
Tel: (0243) 95-03-08
Fax: (0243) 95-68-79
Abbey E-mail: abbaye@solesmes.com
Guesthouse E-mail: hospes@solesmes.com

PLACES TO STAY

WITHIN MONASTERY WALLS

Since the guesthouse is located within the monastic enclosure, only men (either individuals or small groups) may be accommodated for spiritual retreats in silence. Monks can provide counsel if it is desired, and the maximum stay is one week. All guesthouse visitors are expected to assist at the offices. Meals are taken with the monks. During free time, individuals can stroll around certain parts of the monastic grounds, as well as visit the library. All rooms are single occupancy, with sheets and towels provided. Contact the guestmaster prior to your proposed arrival date.

OLD MARBLE FACTORY

Located on monastery property, but not within the monastic enclosure, the Old Marble Factory can accommodate mixed groups of young people in its dormitories. Reservations are difficult to obtain because of the demand, and only those groups of young people with religious motivation can be accommodated. Visitors are expected to assist at most offices.

IN THE VILLAGE OF SOLESMES

Located near the Abbey of Saint Peter is the monastic hotel of Villa Sainte-Anne, which is operated by the Benedictine nuns of Saint Cecilia. Men, women, and children are accepted, and the hotel is open from Palm Sunday to the end of September, as well as at Christmastime. (Groups of twelve or more, however, could possibly be accommodated at other times of the year if prior arrangements have been made.) Villa Sainte-Anne is located about four hundred and fifty yards from the Abbey of Saint Peter, and guests can assist at most of the offices at both abbeys.

TO MAKE RESERVATIONS, CONTACT THE HOTEL AT

Soeur Hotelière
21, rue Jules Alain
72300 Solesmes, France
Tel: (0243) 95-45-05
Fax: (0243) 95-52-01

OTHER ACCOMMODATIONS

Although not operated by either the monks or nuns, there is a hotel located in front of the Abbey of Saint Peter which is open to all people.

FOR MORE INFORMATION, CONTACT THEM AT:

Grand Hotel de Solesmes
Tel: (0243) 95-45-10
Fax: (0243) 95-22-26

DAILY SCHEDULE

10:00 A.M.:	Sung Conventual Mass (1 hour 15 minutes)
	(*Note: Office of Tierce integrated with the Mass)
1:00 P.M.:	Sext (15 minutes)
1:50 P.M.:	None (15 minutes)
5:00 P.M.:	Vespers (30 minutes)
	(*Note: On Thursdays at 4:00 P.M. in summer,
	5:30 P.M. in winter)
8:30 P.M.:	Compline (20 minutes)

The abbey church is open from 9 A.M. to 6 P.M. and for Compline. On Sundays and feast days, it is open from 11:30 A.M. to 6 P.M. A bookstore and an exhibit about the abbey are open—except during religious services—from 11 A.M. to 7 P.M. daily, and from 11:30 A.M. to 7:00 P.M. on Sundays and feast days. Groups wishing to visit the abbey are asked to contact the guestmaster prior to their arrival.

HOW TO REACH SOLESMES

Situated in the western part of France, about one hundred fifty miles from Paris, the abbey of Solesmes stands above the valley of the Sarthe River, almost two miles from the city of Sablé-sur-Sarthe, midway between Le Mans and Angers.

BY ROAD

From Paris, take autoroute A11 West (Paris-Nantes route), exit at Sablé-rur-Sarthe (between Le Mans and Angers), and follow the signs to Solesmes. Another option is to take autoroute A81 (Paris-Rennes route), exit at Brûlon (between Le Mans and Laval), and follow the signs to Solesmes.

BY TRAIN

From Paris, take either the TGV or conventional train from the Montparnasse train station to Le Mans. Change trains at Le Mans (you must purchase a separate ticket) and continue on the train from Le Mans to Sablé-sur-Sarthe. From here, you must either take a taxi or walk to Solesmes, a distance of two miles along the Sarthe River.

From London (Waterloo Station), take the TGV direct to Le Mans (stopping at Lille and Charles de Gaulle Airport but bypassing the city of Paris). Change trains at Le Mans (you must purchase a separate ticket) and continue on the train from Le Mans to Sablé-sur-Sarthe. From here, you must either take a taxi or walk to Solesmes, a distance of two miles along the Sarthe River.

SOLESMES CHANT RECORDINGS & PUBLICATIONS

Chant recordings available from the Abbey of Saint Peter of Solesmes include:

Gregorian Chant Rediscovered
Vespers and Compline
Feasts of Our Lady
Gregorian Sampler
Christmas
Christ in Gethsemane
Maundy Thursday
The Church Sings Her Saints I and II
Tenebrae of Holy Thursday
Tenebrae of Good Friday
Tenebrae of Holy Saturday
Christmas: The Night Office

Requiem Mass
Eastertide
Apostles and Martyrs
Bishops and Doctors
Saint Benedict
Easter
Christmas Night
Chants of Easter
Epiphany & Presentation
Gregorian Requiem
Gregorian Chant: The Monks and Their Music (video)
Solesmes & Dom Guéranger 1805–1875 (book; by Dom Louis Soltner)

CONTACTING THE MONASTERIES, CONVENTS, AND PLACES OF RETREAT

SINCE IT IS very important to make reservations before your arrival with most of the monasteries and convents listed in this book (if you plan to stay overnight), I have provided the necessary information about how to contact and correspond with these various places.

Although every effort has been made to ensure the accuracy of all the information contained in this book, I ask you to please keep in mind that telephone and fax numbers (and even e-mail and Web-site addresses) in Europe change quickly and often. Much of this is due to the rapid development of their communication technologies, but there are several ways to overcome this situation.

If you experience any problems dialing either to telephone or fax numbers, contact the operator and ask to be connected to international dialing assistance. With the name and address of the place you want to contact in hand, an international operator can usually track down the newest city codes and telephone numbers.

Another option, one that will continue to become more effective over time, is to search the Internet for the monastery or convent's name or Web site. As more and more monasteries and convents are joining the World Wide Web with each passing day, it is becoming easier to locate up-to-date information on the Internet.

However, if you are unable to locate a particular monastery or convent's Web site on the Internet, the next best option is to visit the Web site for the monastic order to which they belong. For example, if I wanted some information about a particular Benedictine abbey in Spain, I would first visit the Benedictine Order Web site (www.osb.org) to see if that monastery is listed. If so, there will usually be a direct link to their Web site. If they are not listed, I would then perform a search on the Internet for that particular abbey.

If all else fails, as a last resort, you can contact the national tourist office of the country where it is located. Since the tourist offices usually can be easily found on the Internet, you can either phone, e-mail, or fax them directly with your questions.

When telephoning or faxing a monastery or convent in Europe, here are a few extra things to remember:

- Dial the code number to exit your country
- Dial the code number of the country you are calling
- Dial the city code of the place you are calling
- Dial the local phone number of the place you are calling
- Keep in mind that to dial a number from outside a particular country, you may need to drop the first number (it is usually a zero) of the particular city code. These numbers are used if dialing only from *within the country or area.*
- If writing a letter overseas, always remember to include the country in the mailing address

But what should you include in a letter to a monastery or convent—especially if you are hoping to make a reservation? I recommend including the following:

- Their contact information, including name, mailing address, telephone/fax number, and e-mail address. (Whenever possible, address the letter to the *Guestmaster.*)
- Your contact information, including name, mailing address, telephone/fax number, and e-mail address
- The purpose of your visit (that is, personal spiritual retreat, group spiritual retreat, vocational purposes, and so on)
- The number of people in your group
- Desired dates of arrival and the proposed length of stay
- Gender and ages of the members of your group. (Note: some monasteries/convents accept only men or women, and/or individuals above a certain age.)
- Where applicable, include an official letter from your priest, minister, or rabbi stating your intention to stay overnight at a monastery/convent for spiritual purposes. Although these letters are

required only at a very small minority of places, they can come in handy. (If possible, have the letter translated into the language spoken in the country—or countries—you will be visiting.)
- Always be very respectful, polite, and understanding in your letters. Remember, you are asking to be invited into their homes!

MAKING THE BEST OF YOUR MONASTIC TRAVELS

TO MAKE the best of one's monastic travels, keep in mind the following four ideas:

1. Good Planning
2. Good Research
3. Experiencing the Monastic Life
4. Trusting in Divine Providence

Without a doubt, a fruitful trip always begins with good planning. This includes everything from designing an exciting itinerary, obtaining the necessary travel documents, to buying the right walking shoes and breaking them in several months in advance. A good thing also to keep in mind when mapping out a

"Experiencing the Monastic Life" and trusting in divine Providence are two keys to making the best of your monastic travels.

trip is never to oblige yourself to see everything—or every monastery. Select the places you might like to visit within your allotted time, and then just follow that plan (but do allow for divine Providence to take you elsewhere at times). Otherwise, if you try to visit too many places too quickly, frustration can often set in; you cannot completely absorb each place fully. In fact, the best advice I have ever heard is this: visit just as many places as you are able, and plan on coming back at another time to do the rest (not a bad idea!).

Another vital component of making it a great trip is to do the necessary research beforehand. Especially if you are embarking on a trip to the great monasteries of Europe, it will be to your advantage to learn, in advance, as much as you can about the history of the sites, or about the monastic orders you will be visiting. The more you know about a subject, the more you can derive and profit from it. This book, along with others about the same topic, can provide you with the necessary preliminary groundwork. Of course, as I have previously mentioned, the Internet can also be a valuable tool. It is amazing to see just how much information can be found about monasticism on the World Wide Web. In fact, hundreds of monasteries are joining the Internet with their own Web sites. To help you with this part of your research, I have provided a comprehensive list of monastic-related Web sites in the appendix of this book.

"Experiencing the monastic life" is another key ingredient for a successful and enjoyable trip. No matter how much you plan and research before a trip, if you don't "experience the monastic life" during your travels, everything else can be futile. By "experiencing the monastic life," I mean taking advantage of what each monastery has to offer. By attending the services, walking the grounds, speaking with the monks (if and when appropriate), enjoying the silence, participating in the schedule of the abbey, and praying (yes, praying), you can then begin to get a true sense of what monastic life is all about. By doing this, you can gain a much deeper appreciation of the places you will be visiting, and the people you will meet.

The most important element, however, of any monastic trip, is handing over the reigns of your life to God and trusting in divine Providence. Although this may sometimes be the most difficult part of the journey, it is always the most rewarding. By abandoning yourself to divine Providence, you open yourself up to the unknown, yet exciting, plans of God. It is because of divine Providence that many apparent travel "mishaps," such as missed or rerouted trains, can turn into incredible blessings. At every bend and turn, there are new friends to meet, new places to see, and new experiences to behold. During my travels backpacking through eighteen European countries, it was amazing just how many times "detoured plans" turned into unexpected highlights. That's how I learned about places such as Solesmes, Santo Domingo de Silos, Montserrat, Fontgombault, Klosterneuburg, Heiligenkreuz, and Kalwaria Zebrzydowska—all monasteries and abbeys listed in this book. Trusting in God's divine Providence during our travels is not always easy, but it does allow us to advance in our faith—and that is the purpose of a monastic pilgrimage.

Part 3

Europe's Monastery &
Convent Guesthouses

SPECIAL NOTE

To view maps representing the locations of the
monasteries and convents, you can visit the Web site
www:catholicadventures.com.

AUSTRIA

$$\boxed{\begin{matrix} + & + \\ + & + \end{matrix}}$$

Benediktinerstift

3591 Altenburg (Bez Horn)
Tel: (02982) 34-51, 34-51-21 • Fax: (02982) 34-51-13
E-mail: kultur.tourismus@stift-altenburg.at
Web Site: www.stift-altenburg.at

Founded in 1144, today the Altenburg Abbey is home to a community of Benedictine monks. Visitors can tour the imposing abbey church which features a number of beautiful frescoes, sculptures, and other religious artwork. All are invited to participate in the daily prayer life of the monks, as well as attend the many summer concerts. Even though only men can be accommodated in the monastery's comfortable guesthouse, the abbey's restaurant and gift shop are open to everyone.

Benediktinerabtei Saint Georgenberg

6130 Fiecht (Schwaz)
Tel: (05242) 632-76-37 • Fax: (05242) 632-76-33
Web Site: www.st-georgenberg.at

Founded in 1138, today the Abbey of Saint Georgenberg is home to a community of Benedictine monks. Mass is celebrated daily, with the March 19 feast day of Saint Joseph (the patron of the abbey church) receiving the largest number of visitors annually. The monastery operates a large guesthouse for both men and women, with approximately seventy beds available.

Stift Göttweig

3511 Furth bei Göttweig (Krems)
Tel: (02732) 855-81 • Fax: (02732) 855-81-244
E-mail: koloman@via.at; goettweig@kloesterreich.at
Web Site: www.stiftgoettweig.at

Among the many monasteries of Austria, the Benedictine Abbey of Göttweig remains one of the most famous. Dating from 1065, the abbey has long served as a major place of pilgrimage

because of its reputation as a hub for culture, art, religion, architecture, and warm hospitality. Perched above a hill with breathtaking views of the world-famous Danube valley below, Göttweig continues to welcome visitors from all over the world who come to tour its abbey, cloister, crypt, museum, art collections, and exhibitions. All are welcome to attend the monks' vesper services, as well as Mass. The monastery also operates a restaurant serving specialties from the regional cuisine. A guesthouse is available, but reservations must be made in advance as rooms are very limited.

Saint Hemma Gästehaus
Domkustodie Salvatorianerkolleg
9342 Gurk
Tel: (04266) 8236, (04266) 8557-0 • Fax: (04266) 8236-16
E-mail: dom.zu.gurk@happynet.at

Founded in 1043 by Saint Hemma, this monastery is home to a community of Salvatorian fathers and brothers. Attracting visitors from throughout Europe and abroad, this pilgrimage site features the tomb of Saint Hemma, as well as a number of beautiful religious artworks housed in the Episcopal Chapel. Guided tours of the sanctuary are available. The Salvatorians operate a comfortable guesthouse, which is open to both men and women.

Zisterzienserstift Heiligenkreuz
2532 Heiligenkreuz bei Baden
Tel: (02258) 87-03 • Fax: (02258) 87-03-114
E-mail: information@stift-heiligenkreuz.at
Web Site: www.stift-heiligenkreuz.at

Founded in 1133, the Heiligenkreuz Abbey is home to a community of about fifty Cistercian monks. Visitors can participate in the prayer life of the monks by attending the Liturgy of the Hours and Mass, both of which are sung in Gregorian chant. The monastery guesthouse provides different types of accommodations, making it suitable for both independent travelers (up to twenty-five people) and groups of young adults (two dormitory-style rooms with thirty to forty bunk beds).

Augustiner Chorherrenstift

3130 Herzogenburg (Sankt Pölten)
Tel/Fax: (02782) 831-13
E-mail: stift@herzogenburg.at, stift-fuehrungen@herzogenburg.at
Web Site: www.herzogenburg.at/stift

Founded in 1244, today the Abbey of Augustiner Chorherrenstift is home to a community of Augustinian monks. Mass is celebrated daily in the abbey church, which all visitors are welcome to attend. Guest rooms are available; however, one must reserve them in advance by writing or sending a fax directly to the abbey. Several of the monastery's wines may be purchased at the gift shop.

Bildungshaus der Serviten

Maria Luggau
9655 Maria Luggau
Tel: (04716) 601 • Fax: (04716) 601-17

A place of pilgrimage since 1513, Maria Luggau receives several thousand visitors each year who come to pray before a miraculous image of the Virgin Mary. In the nineteenth century, the Servite Fathers built a monastery here, near the

shrine, to take care of the pilgrims' needs. Today, the Servites continue their role of providing hospitality by operating a very large and comfortable guesthouse which accommodates approximately sixty-five people (five singles, thirty doubles).

Benediktinerstift Melk

Abt-Berthold-Dietmayr Straße 1
3390 Melk
Tel: (02752) 523-12-225 • Fax: (02752) 523-12-226
E-mail: kultur.tourismus@stiftmelk.at
Web Site: www.stiftmelk.at

Founded more than nine hundred years ago, throughout the centuries, the Melk Abbey has served as one of Austria's most important spiritual and cultural centers. Home to a community of Benedictine monks, the monastery welcomes thousands of visitors annually who come to tour its immense complex. Guided tours of the abbey's church, library, and grounds are available. A guesthouse is available for men; however, reservations can be very difficult to obtain.

Prämonstratenser ChorherrenStiftes Schlägl

4160 Schlägl 1 (Aigen im Mühlkreis)
Tel: (07281) 8801-0 • Fax: (07281) 8801-227

Founded in 1218, the Abbey Schlägl is a monastery of the Order of Premonstratensians, also known as the Norbertine Fathers. The monks are devoted to a number of apostolic activities including parish work, catechesis and teaching, education, science, culture, and economic involvement. The abbey runs a large seminar center, which is used as a place for meditation, meetings, and educational classes. For its participants, the center offers forty-beds, seminar rooms, a meditation room, and a number of other facilities.

Stift Schlierbach

4533 Schlierbach (Inzersdorf)
Tel: (07582) 83-013 • Fax: (07582) 83-013-176

Founded in 1355, today the Schlierbach Abbey is home to a community of Cistercian monks. Visitors can take guided tours of the monastery, as well as attend daily Mass with the monks. A comfortable guesthouse is available for those individuals and groups seeking a place for prayer and silence. Visitors and guests can dine in the abbey restaurant (Stiftskeller), and purchase the delicious "monastery-made" cheeses in the gift shop. A number of concerts and art exhibitions take place at the abbey each year.

Benediktinerabtei Seckau

Abteiverwaltung
8732 Seckau 1
Tel: (03514) 52-34-0, 5234-101 • Fax: (03514) 52-34-105
E-mail: verwaltung@abtei-seckau.at
Web Site: www.abtei-seckau.at

Founded in 1140, the Abbey of Seckau is home to a community of Benedictine monks. A very prominent monastery throughout the ages, visitors are welcome to tour the immense abbey grounds and church—both of which feature numerous works of art and grand architecture. All are also invited to attend religious services with the monks, which includes the Liturgy of the Hours and Mass. Even though only men can be accommodated in the guesthouse (which is located within the monastic enclosure), other individuals and couples can be accommodated in the Hotel Hofwirt which is located on the abbey grounds.

Stift Seitenstetten

Am Klosterberg 1
3353 Seitenstetten
Tel: (07477) 423-00, 423-00-38 • Fax: (07477) 423-00-50
E-mail: stift@stift-seitenstetten.at
Guesthouse E-mail: papepi@stift-seitenstetten.at
Web Site: www.stift-seitenstetten.at

Founded in 1112, the Abbey of Seitenstetten is home to a community of Benedictine monks. Guided tours of the monastery grounds, church, cloister, library, and museum are available. Throughout the year, a number of seminars, conferences, and retreats take place at the abbey. The monastery operates a small guesthouse of seven rooms with thirteen beds. There is a gift shop

on the premises which sells religious books, CDs, tapes, liquor, and other products of the abbey. There is also a guesthouse located on the exterior of the monastery, which can provide accommodations for up to twenty-six people. They can be contacted at: Bildungszentrum Saint Benedikt, Promenade 13, 3353 Seitenstetten, Tel: (07477) 42885, Fax: (07477) 42885-20.

Schottenabtei

Freyung 6
1010 Vienna
Tel: (1) 534-98-0 • Fax: (1) 534-98-105
E-mail: schotten@schottenstift.at
Web Site: www.schottenstift.at

Founded almost eight centuries ago, the Abbey of Schotten is home to a community of Benedictine monks. Located in the heart of Vienna, visitors are welcome to attend religious services with the monks and tour their museum. The monks operate a very comfortable guesthouse called Saint Benediktushaus (Saint Benedict House). To make reservations, contact them at: Saint Benediktushaus, Freyung 6a, 1010 Vienna, Guesthouse Tel: (1) 534-98-905, 534-98-900, Guesthouse Fax: (1) 534-98-12.

Chorherren Stift Vorau

8250 Vorau (Graz)
Tel: (03337) 281-54, (03337) 235-10

Originally founded in 1237, today the Abbey of Chorherren Vorau is home to a community of Augustinian monks. Mass is celebrated daily, and all visitors are welcome to participate in religious services with the monks in the abbey church. Sixteen comfortable guest rooms are available for those visitors who seek a place for personal prayer and retreat. Many seminars and conferences take place at the abbey throughout the year.

Bildungshaus Stift Zwettl

3910 Zwettl
Tel: (02822) 550-0, 550-57 • Fax: (02822) 550-50
Abbey (Information) E-mail: info@stift-zwettl.co.at
Guesthouse E-mail: bildungshaus@stift-zwettl.co.at
Web Site: www.stift-zwettl.co.at

Founded in the twelfth century, the Abbey of Zwettl is home to a community of Cistercian monks. Located in the countryside of the northern region of Austria, the monastery has long attracted visitors because of its rich history and tradition, and for its magnificent church— often referred to as "a royal cathedral in Cistercian Guise." Pilgrims and tourists can visit the abbey, pray in the church, and take contemplative walks in the nearby fields. The abbey operates both a large guesthouse and restaurant. (Be sure to visit the abbey Web site which features a live video-cam!).

Abbaye Notre–Dame–du–Val–Dieu

Rue Val-Dieu 227
4880 Aubel
Tel: (087) 68-73-81, 68-74-02 • Fax: (087) 68-69-83

Founded in 1216, the Abbey of Notre-Dame-du-Val-Dieu is home to a community of Cistercian monks. Visitors are invited to attend religious services with the monks, including Mass and the Liturgy of the Hours. With more than twenty guest rooms available, both individuals and groups are welcome to stay for several days of prayer and reflection. Young people traveling together are invited to participate in the prayer life of the monastery, as special accommodations are available for them. Abbey cheeses, religious artwork, and music tapes can be purchased at the gift shop. Concerts and conferences which take place throughout the year at the monastery are open to the public.

Abbaye des Prémontrés

2, rue A. De Moor
1421 Bois-Seigneur-Isaac
Tel: (067) 21-24-73 • Fax: (067) 21-43-22

In 1413, the Order of Regular Canons of Saint Augustine built a monastery here to welcome the thousands of pilgrims who would come annually to venerate a Eucharistic Miracle dating back to 1405. In 1903, the members of the Order of the Premonstratensians from Mondaye (Calvados, France) took over the abbey. They gave it to their Belgian counterparts in 1921. Today, the monks operate a guesthouse with eleven rooms (reservations required three weeks in advance), as well as a gift shop which sells many items related to the Eucharistic Miracle. French, Dutch, English, and Italian are spoken by the monks.

Abbaye Notre-Dame-de-Clairefontaine

Cordemois
6830 Bouillon
Tel: (061) 46-61-59 • Fax: (061) 46-63-76
E-mail: abbaye.clairefontaine@skynet.be

Founded in 1845, today the Abbey of Notre-Dame-de-Clairfontaine is home to a community of Trappist monks. Visitors are welcome to attend religious services with the monks, which includes Mass and the Liturgy of the Hours (both of which are sung or said in French). Twenty guest rooms are available for those individuals who seek a personal or group retreat in a monastic setting of prayer and silence. With a bakery on the premises, visitors can purchase the abbey's own breads and cookies.

Sint Andriesabdij Van Zevenkerken

Abbaye de Saint-André
Zevenkerken 4
8200 Saint Andries (Brugge 2)
Tel: (050) 38-01-36 • Fax: (050) 38-79-60

Founded in 1902, the Abbey of Saint André is home to a community of Benedictine monks. Visitors are welcome to attend Mass (recited in Dutch) in the chapel, and individuals who seek a time for personal prayer and contemplation can ask to stay in one of the guest rooms. Ceramics and religious icons made by the monks may be purchased in the abbey gift shop.

Monasterium de Wijngaard

Monastery of the Vineyard
Begijnhof 24-30
8000 Brugge
Tel: (050) 33-00-11 • Fax: (050) 33-18-81

Founded in 1927, the Monastery of the Vineyard is home to a community of Benedictine nuns. Central to the life of the sisters is the Mass and Liturgy of the Hours, both of which are sung in Gregorian chant. The priory has a guesthouse where women, girls, and married couples can come to rest, pray, relax, or study (for a minimum of three days). Another attraction at the monastery is the Beguine museum.

Monastère de Chevetogne

5590 Chevetogne
Tel: (083) 21-17-63 • Fax: (083) 21-60-45
E-mail: abbaye@monasterechevetogne.com
Web Site: www.monasterechevetogne.com

Founded in the 1920s, the Monastery of Chevetogne is comprised of a community of Benedictine monks who are organized into two liturgical groups, and celebrate according to both the Latin and the Byzantine Rites. The monastery has three separate guesthouses which are open to receive individuals and groups who want to make a retreat and share in the prayer life of the monks (each guesthouse is designated to receive either men, women, or groups). Since there is both a Latin and Byzantine church, guests are encouraged to join the monks for the daily Divine Office in both rites. The abbey's CDs of Slavonic liturgical chants are available for purchase, along with their many icons and books.

Abbaye Notre-Dame-de-la-Paix

1, chaussée de Trélon
6460 Chimay
Tel: (060) 21-11-64 • Fax: (060) 21-49-36

Founded in 1207, today the Abbey of Notre-Dame-de-la-Paix is home to a community of Trappist monks. Visitors are welcome to participate in the prayer life of the monks, which includes Mass and the Liturgy of the Hours. About twelve guest rooms are available to those individuals and groups who wish to experience the monastic life more fully. Religious vestments, hosts, and the abbey's beer may be purchased at the gift shop. The monastery is located near the Abbey of Scourmont, which is known for its famous Trappist Beer production.

Abbaye de Maredsous

5537 Denée
Tel: (082) 69-82-11 • Fax: (082) 69-83-21, (082) 69-82-21
E-mail: webmaster@maredsous.com
Web Site: www.maredsous.com

Founded in 1872, the Benedictine Abbey of Maredsous was the first monastery constructed in Belgium after the French Revolution. The monks operate a thirty-room guesthouse, which is open to both men and women who seek a time of spiritual renewal and prayer. A cafeteria is located on the premises. Among the most popular items sold at the abbey gift shop are the cheeses and beers produced by the monks.

Abbaye Notre-Dame-de-Leffe
1, place de l'Abbaye
5500 Dinant
Tel: (082) 22-23-77 • Fax: (082) 21-37-28

Founded in 1152, the Abbey of Notre-Dame-de-Leffe is home to a community of Premonstratensians (Norbertine Fathers). When visiting the monastery, individuals can ask to take a tour of the abbey and its grounds (only certain parts of the cloister, however, are open to the public). All are welcome to attend religious services with the monks, which includes Mass, the Liturgy of the Hours, and Eucharistic Adoration. Groups seeking a spiritual retreat may be accommodated in the abbey guesthouse.

Monastère Notre-Dame
Rue du Monastère
5644 Ermeton-sur-Biert
Tel: (071) 72-00-40 • Information: (071) 72-00-48
Fax: (071) 72-73-92
E-mail: monastere.ermeton@skynet.be

Founded in 1917, the Monastery of Notre-Dame is home to a women's community of Benedictine monks. As well as visiting the ancient chapel and castle, the faithful can participate in the prayer life of the monks, which includes Mass and the Divine Office (in French). The abbey operates a guesthouse, which features more than twenty-eight rooms, receiving both men and women (families with infants can also be accommodated).

Carmel de Sainte–Thérèse de Jésus

5, rue du Carmel
5150 Floreffe
Tel: (081) 44-43-64 • Fax: (081) 44-61-64

Founded in 1860, the Convent of Sainte-Thérèse de Jésus is home to a community of Carmelite nuns. Mass is celebrated daily, along with the Divine Office, both of which are open to all visitors. Individuals seeking a time of personal retreat may be accommodated in the convent guest rooms.

Abbaye Notre–Dame–de–Scourmount

6464 Forges
Tel: (060) 21-30-63, 21-05-11 • Fax: (060) 21-40-18, 21-36-96
E-mail: abbaye@scourmont.be
Web Site: www.scourmont.be

Founded in 1850, today the Abbey of Notre-Dame-de-Scourmount is home to a community of about twenty Trappist monks. All visitors are welcome to join the monks in their religious services, including the daily celebration of Mass and Vespers. Even though there are a small number of guest rooms available, individuals seeking a time of prayer and solitude may be accommodated.

Saint Benedictus Abdij De Achelse Kluis

De Kluis 1
3930 Hamont-Aachel
Tel (Abbey): (011) 800-760 • Tel (Guesthouse): (011) 800-766
Fax: (011) 648-130
E-mail: abdij@achelsekluis.myweb.nl
Web Site: www.achelsekluis.be

Founded in 1686, the Abbey of Achelse Kluis is home to a community of Cistercian monks. Serving as a place of prayer and contemplation, the monastery invites all visitors to join them in the chapel for Mass and the singing of the Divine Office. The monastery

guesthouse receives both men and women, and provides an opportunity for individuals to join the monks in their prayerful rhythm of life.

Monastère de Marie-Médiatrice
24, rue du Saint-Esprit
1540 Herne
Tel: (02) 396-17-43

Founded in 1926, today the Monastery of Mary Mediatrix is home to a community of Dominican monks of the Rosary. Visitors are welcome to attend religious services with the monks, which includes Mass and the Liturgy of the Hours (in French). The monks operate a guesthouse called the "House of Prayer" which can receive both men and women who seek a time of prayer and silence.

Abdij Keizersberg (Abbaye du Mont-César)
Mechelsestraat 202
3000 Leuven
Tel: (016) 310-060 • Fax: (016) 310-066

Founded in 1899, the Abbey of Keizersberg is home to a community of Benedictine monks. Every day visitors can attend the religious services of the monastery, which includes Mass and the Liturgy of the Hours (both are sung in Dutch and Gregorian chant). Guest-room accommodations are available for those individuals who wish to partake in the monastic prayer life of the abbey. Beer and cheese are two of the major products produced by the abbey, both of which can be purchased at the gift shop.

Abbaye-de-la-Paix-Notre-Dame-d'Averbode
Boulevard d'Avroy, 54
4000 Liège
Tel: (04) 223-77-20 • Fax: (04) 223-35-80
E-mail: abbaye.pnd@swing.be

Founded in 1627, the Abbey of Paix-Notre-Dame is home to a community of Benedictine monks. While visiting, the faithful can participate in the prayer life of the monks (Mass and the Liturgy of the Hours are said/sung in French). Many conferences and organized retreats are held at the guesthouse throughout the year. Both individuals and groups can be accommodated in the abbey guesthouse. Specialists in painting, the monks sell some of their creations—including jewelry, china dishes, scarves, clothing, and religious icons —at the gift shop.

Monastère Notre-Dame-de-Béthanie

8, Sysen
8210 Loppem-Zedelgem
Tel: (050) 38-31-71 • Fax: (050) 38-82-74

Founded in 1921, the Monastery of Notre-Dame-de-Béthanie is home to a women's community of Benedictine monks. Visitors are invited to attend the daily recitation of the Divine Office (sung in Dutch), as well as Mass on Sundays. Guest rooms are available for those individuals and groups who wish to embark on a personal or group retreat in a prayerful atmosphere.

Monastère Clarté Notre-Dame

41, rue des Monastères
5020 Malonne
Tel: (081) 44-47-40 • Fax: (081) 45-02-67
E-mail: clarissesmalonne@swing.be

Founded in 1903, the Monastery of Clarté Notre-Dame is home to a community of Poor Clare nuns. The Liturgy of the Hours, which is celebrated daily in French, is open to all visitors. The monastery operates a guesthouse for those individuals or groups who wish to spend a few days in a monastic retreat (thirteen guest rooms are available). Visitors who stay overnight in the guesthouse may be asked to help work in the garden.

Monastère de Bethléem

Notre-Dame-des-Sources-Vives
5024, Marche-les-Dames
Tel: (081) 58-99-07

Originally founded as a Cistercian abbey in the thirteenth century, today the Monastery of Bethléem is home to a community of Bethlehem monks. Visitors can attend religious services with the monks in the abbey church (Mass and the Liturgy of the Hours are said in French). Individuals wishing to partake in the monastic life may be accommodated in the guesthouse, but they must strictly adhere to the silent and prayerful atmosphere of the abbey. Religious articles and products made by the monks may be purchased.

Abbaye de Maredret

5537 Maredret
Tel: (082) 69-91-34, 69-91-45 • Fax: (082) 69-90-89

Founded in 1893, the Abbey of Maredret is home to a women's community of Benedictine monks. Visitors can attend the Divine Office and Mass with the monks, both of which are sung in French and Gregorian chant. Guesthouse accommodations are available for those individuals and small groups who wish to undertake a monastic retreat. A guided tour of the abbey church is available upon request.

Abbey de Postel

Norbertijnenabdij Postel (Abbaye Norbertine)
Abdijlaan, 16
2400 Mol-Postel
Tel: (014) 37-81-21, 37-81-23 • Fax: (014) 37-81-23
E-mail: postula@skynet.be

Founded in 1140, the Abbey of Postel is home to a community of Canons Regular of Premonstratensians (Norbertine Fathers). As well as exploring the twelfth-century church, visitors can participate in the prayer life of the monks by attending Mass and the Liturgy of the Hours. Guest rooms are available for those individuals who wish to embark on a personal or group retreat in a monastic setting. Dutch, French, German, and English are spoken at the abbey. The monks operate a large farm and a famous dairy.

Monastère Saint–André–de–Clerlande

1, Allée de Clerlande
1340 Ottignies
Tel: (010) 41-74-63 • Fax: (010) 41-80-27

Founded in 1971, the Monastery of Saint-André-de-Clerlande is home to a community of Benedictine monks. Individuals, couples, and groups (no larger than ten people) are welcome to stay in the guesthouse. One of the major apostolates of the monks is the making of religious icons.

Monastère de l'Alliance

64, rue Albert-1er
1330 Rixensart
Tel: (02) 652-06-01 • Fax: (02) 652-06-46
E-mail: benedictines.rixensart@skynet.be

Founded in 1968, the Monastery of the Alliance is home to a community of Benedictine monks. The Liturgy of the Hours is recited in the abbey church (in French), and all visitors are welcome to attend. A guesthouse with twenty-four rooms is available to those individuals who wish to participate more fully in the prayer life of the monastery.

Notre–Dame–d'Hurtebise

2, rue du Monastère
6870 Saint-Hubert
Tel: (061) 61-11-27 • Fax: (061) 61-32-76

Founded in 1938, the Abbey of Notre-Dame-d'Hurtebise is home to a community of Benedictine monks. While visiting the monastery, the faithful can participate in religious services with the monks, which includes the Liturgy of the Hours and Mass (recited in French). Individuals seeking a few days of retreat can ask to be accommodated in the abbey guesthouse.

Priorij Regina Pacis

Sint-Amelbergalei 35
2900 Schoten
Tel: (03) 658-44-68 • Fax: (03) 658-83-01
E-mail: benedictinessen.schoten@skynet.be or
priorij.schotenhof@monasteria.org
Web Site: www.benedictinessen-schoten.be

Founded in 1879, today the Priory of Regina Pacis is home to a women's community of Benedictine monks. Visitors can attend the daily Mass and Liturgy of the Hours, both of which are celebrated in the abbey church. Once a month, a Byzantine Rite Mass is also celebrated, which is open to all. Guest rooms are available for those individuals who wish to participate more fully in the prayer life of the monastery.

Monastère Saint-Remacle

Wavreumont
4970 Stavelot
Tel: (080) 86-23-18 • Fax: (080) 88-01-82

Founded in 1950, the Monastery of Saint-Remacle is home to a community of Benedictine monks. Mass and the Liturgy of the Hours are celebrated daily (in French), all visitors are welcome to participate. The monastery operates a guesthouse which provides accommodations for those individuals seeking a time of prayer and silence.

Abbaye d'Orval

6823 Villers-devant-Orval
Tel (Guesthouse): (061) 32-51-10 • Tel (Switchboard): (061) 31-10-60
Fax (Guesthouse): (061) 32-51-36 • Fax (Abbey): (061) 31-55-95
E-mail (Abbaye): econome@orval.be
Web Site: www.orval.be

First founded by Benedictine monks in 1070, Orval Abbey was later refounded by the Trappist Cistercian monks in the twelfth century. Although the monks are involved in a number of economic activities to support their livelihood, they have become best known for their beer and cheese throughout the world. In fact, Orval is only one of six breweries in the world that is allowed to have their beer designated a "Trappist" product—a strictly controlled mark of quality. Individuals and groups who are looking for a time of spiritual renewal, as well as personal and community prayer, are invited to spend time on retreat in the monastic guesthouse (for periods from two to  seven days). Visitors can tour parts of the ruins of the old abbey (12th-13th century), enter its underground museum, and view an audiovisual presentation about the monastery.

Norbertijnenabdij Tongerlo
(Abbaye Norbertine de Tongerlo)

Abdijstraat 40
2260 Tongerlo-Westerlo
Tel: (014) 53-99-00 • Fax: (014) 53-99-08
E-mail: abdij@tongerlo.org
Web Site: www.tongerlo.org

Originally founded in 1130, today the Abbey of Tongerlo is home to a community of Canons Regular of Premonstratensians (Norbertine Fathers). Visitors can tour the abbey church, museum, and attend the Divine Office and Mass with the monks (sung in Dutch). Individuals interested in participating more fully in the life of the monastery can be accommodated in one of the abbey's guest rooms. Dutch and French are spoken at the abbey. Bread, cheese, butter, and beer produced by the monks may be purchased at the gift shop. Every year, on November 14, a large pilgrimage to the monastery takes place in honor of Saint Siard.

Abbaye de Westmalle

Abdij der Trappisten
2390 Westmalle
Tel: (033) 12-92-00, 12-92-22 • Fax: (033) 12-92-28, 12-92-20
E-mail: info@trappistwestmalle.be
Web Site: www.trappistwestmalle.be

Founded in 1794, the Abbey of Notre-Dame du Sacré Coeur is home to a community of Trappist monks. World famous for their cheese and beer, people from all over the globe come to visit the abbey. All are welcome to attend the Liturgy of the Monks and Mass, both of which are sung in Dutch. Since guest rooms are limited, only those individuals who wish to undertake a personal retreat of prayer and silence can be accommodated.

Saint Sixtus–Abdij

Abbaye Notre-Dame-de-Saint-Sixte
12, Donkerstraat
8640 Westvleteren
Tel: (057) 40-03-76 • Tel (Guesthouse): (057) 40-19-70
Fax: (057) 40-14-20

Originally founded in 1260 (or even possibly as early as 806), today the Abbey of Notre-Dame-de-Saint-Sixte is home to a community of Trappist monks. Only those individuals or groups staying in the guesthouse can attend the Divine Office and Mass with the monks. You must contact the abbey in advance to inquire about the possibility of reserving a guest room. It is essential for all individuals who wish to stay in the guesthouse overnight to have, as their sole intention, a visit to the abbey for the purpose of a retreat. They must also maintain a prayerful and silent attitude. Along with monasteries such as those at Orval, Westmalle, and Chival, the Abbey of Notre Dame de Saint-Sixte is one of only six breweries who have the right to produce "Trappist" beer.

Samostan Sv. Petra Ap.

Jadranska Obala 17
51557 Cres
Tel: (051) 571-010

Founded in 1200, Samostan Sv. Petra Abbey is home to a small community of Benedictine monks. Although the feast days of Saint Peter (June 29) and Saint Benedict (March 21 and July 11) remain the most important days of celebration at the abbey, visitors are welcome to join the monks in daily religious services in the monastery chapel. Individuals and small groups seeking a spiritual retreat can be accommodated in the abbey guest rooms.

Benediktinci Cokovac

Tkon
23212 Tkon (Pasman)
Tel/Fax: (023) 85-771

Founded in 1125, today the Monastery of Cokovac is home to a community of Benedictine monks. As well as exploring the beautiful fourteenth-century Gothic church, the faithful can participate in the prayer life of the monks, which includes Mass and the Liturgy of the Hours. During the summer, classical music concerts take place at the abbey. Since the guesthouse is very small (four rooms), only men can be accommodated.

Kláster premonstrátu

Klásterní hospic
36461 Teplá u Touzime
Tel: (0169) 392-691 • Fax: (0169) 392-634
E-mail: klaster.tepla@mbox.apsa.cz

Founded in the thirteenth century, the Tepla Abbey is home to a community of Premonstratensian monks who are attempting to restore the grand monastery following years of devastation. On July 17, 1993, the abbey consecrated a new guesthouse for visitors which can accommodate about one hundred people, and is also home to a large restaurant and mini-brewery. Guests can attend the Liturgy of the Hours sung by the monastic choir and take a guided tour of the abbey, which includes a visit to the monastery's vast library—recognized as the second largest in all of Central Europe.

DENMARK

$$\begin{array}{c}+\|+\\ \overline{\|}\\ +\|+\end{array}$$

Maria Hertje Kloster (Heart of Mary Abbey)

Maria Hertje Engen
8500 Grenaa
Tel: (04586) 38-44-88 • Fax: (04586) 38-42-06

Founded in 1961, the Heart of Mary Priory (elevated to the status of Abbey in 1998) is a contemplative community of Cistercian Nuns, dedicated to praying for the world with the whole Church. Since their community has grown considerably in the past twenty years, the nuns recently built a new convent (in the traditional Cistercian style). It was consecrated on May 29, 1992. Guests can attend the daily singing of the nuns' Liturgy of the Hours in the new abbey church. To inquire about staying overnight at the guesthouse, contact them at the following address: Guest House and Course Centre, Sostrup Slot (Castle), Maria Hjerte Engen, 8500 Grenaa, Denmark, Tel: (04586) 38-41-11, Fax: (04586) 38-41-33.

+‖+
+‖+

The Reception Office

The Friars
Aylesford, Kent ME20 7BX
Tel: (01622) 71-72-72 • Fax: (01622) 71-55-75
E-mail: friarsreception@hotmail.com, friarsevents@hotmail.com
Web Site: www.carmelite.org/aylesford

Founded in 1242, Aylesford Priory is home to a community of Carmelite friars. According to tradition, this is where the Blessed Virgin Mary revealed the famous Brown Scapular to Saint Simon Stock (the prior general of the order at that time). A very popular place of pilgrimage, Aylesford welcomes pilgrims from all over the world who come to explore the abbey grounds and engage in either personal or group retreats. Very well equipped to receive large numbers of people, the priory has extensive conference facilities for religious groups, educational courses, and business groups. There is a program of retreats arranged by the Carmelite community, and everyone is welcome to join in the prayer life of the friars. The abbey guesthouse can accommodate up to one hundred people in single or double rooms. Anyone wishing to bring a group should contact the pilgrimage secretary prior to their arrival.

Belmont Abbey of Saint Michael & All Angels

Belmont, Hereford HR2 9RZ
Tel: (01432) 277-388 • Fax: (01432) 277-597
E-mail: procoffice@aol.com
Web Site: www.belmontabbey.org.uk

Founded in 1859, the Belmont Abbey is a member of the English Benedictine Congregation, which is currently the oldest of the twenty-one

Benedictine Congregations throughout the world, claiming continuity with the Congregations established in the thirteenth century by the Holy See. Recognized as the second largest English Benedictine House in England, the abbey operates a very comfortable and well-established guesthouse (Hedley Lodge), which accommodates up to forty people. Both private and guided retreats are available for either individuals and/or groups. As well as operating the guesthouse and its Common Novitiate (House of Studies), the Belmont monks serve in most of the Catholic parishes in the surrounding area.

Buckfast Abbey

Buckfastleigh, Devon TQ11 0EE
Tel: (01364) 643-301, 642-519 • Fax: (01364) 643-891
E-mail: enquiries@buckfast.org.uk
Web Site: www.buckfast.org.uk

Originally founded in 1018 by the Cistercians, Buckfast Abbey was later refounded in 1882 by a community of Benedictine monks. Renowned for its history and architecture, the monastery provides a wealth of activities to do and sites to see for the visitor: the abbey church, Medieval Guest Hall, gardens, video presentations, and a gift and monastic produce shop. Southgate is the monastic retreat house which can accommodate up to twenty people for individual or group retreats. In addition to Southgate, there are some guest rooms in the monastery itself which are available to men who come on their own: they can apply to the guestmaster to stay in one of them.

Prinknash Abbey

Cranham, Gloucester GL4 8EX
Tel: (01452) 812-455 • Fax: (01452) 812-529, 812-066
Web Sites: http://web.ukonline.co.uk/david.w34/_prinknash.html
www.prinknashabbey.org.uk

Founded in the 1890s, today Prinknash Abbey is home to a community of about thirty Benedictine monks. As a means to support itself, the monastery operates a farm and garden, and distributes its world-renowned pottery and incense around the globe. The abbey farm is a zoolike park that features numerous animals, including birds, deer and various waterfowl—perfect for families and children. Visitors are welcome to spend time in the monastic retreat house.

Saint Mary's Priory

Fernham
Faringdon, Oxfordshire SN7 7PP
E-mail: fernhampriory@btinternet.com
Web Site: www.btinternet.com/~fernhampriory/index.htm

Although the earliest days of the Benedictine community dates back to the sixth century, the actual founding of Saint Mary's Priory was in the eighteenth century. In 1991, the nuns opened Saint Gabriel's Retreat House, which receives both men and women who wish to spend time in silence and prayer. All are invited to join the sisters in the Liturgy of the Hours. It is interesting to note that Saint Mary's Priory has never aspired to the status of abbey, and has accepted the Virgin Mary as their Abbess.

Saint Michael's Abbey

280 Farnborough Road
Farnborough, Hampshire GU14 7NQ
Tel: (01252) 546-105 • Fax: (01252) 372-822
Web Site: www.farnboroughabbey.org

Founded in 1887, Saint Michael's Abbey is home to a community of Benedictine monks. As well as attending religious services in the monastery, visitors can spend time touring the spectacular abbey church. Ten guest rooms (nine singles, one double) are available, but are only open to men and/or young people who desire to partake in the prayer life of the community. Among the monks' main apostolic works is the restoration of ancient books and the production of vestments and religious icons.

Ealing Abbey

Charlbury Grove
London, W5 2DY
Tel: (0181) 862-2100 • Fax: (0181) 862-2199
Web Site: http://members.aol.com/ealingmonk

Founded in 1897, Ealing Abbey is located in the heart of west London, and is home to a community of Benedictine monks. As well as prayer, the main apostolic duty of the monks includes parish work, running a school, and offering spiritual retreats and courses. Visitors may join the monastic community in their daily prayers, for a meal, or even stay overnight in one of their guest rooms.

Saint Mildred's Abbey

Minster-in-Thanet
Nr Ramsgate
Kent CT12 4HF
Tel: (01843) 821-254

Founded in 1050, Saint Mildred's Abbey is home to a community of Benedictine monks. Visitors are invited to attend religious services with the monks and pray before the relics of Saint Mildred in the monastery church. A guesthouse, which is open during the spring and summer, is available to those individuals and groups who wish to participate more fully in the prayer life of the abbey. The monks also operate an excellent restaurant, which is open to all visitors.

Saint Augustine's Abbey

Saint Augustine's Road
Ramsgate
Kent CT11 9PA
Fax: (01843) 582-732

Founded in 1856, Saint Augustine's Abbey is home to a community of Benedictine monks. All visitors are welcome to participate in religious services with the monks, which includes Mass and the Liturgy of the Hours. Six guest rooms are available for those men who come with a desire to spend time in prayer and silence. The monks' apostolic work includes the production of liturgical vestments and ornaments.

Saint Cecilia's Abbey

Ryde, Isle of Wight PO33 1LH
Tel/Fax: (01983) 562-602

Founded in 1882, the women's monastery of Saint Cecilia became a part of the Solesmes Congregation in 1950. Services are sung daily in Gregorian chant by the Benedictine nuns, and guests can follow along using the Liturgy of the Hours books which are provided (translations are in English). Adjacent to the abbey is the Garth Retreat House, which provides accommodation for men and women who wish to spend several days in a monastic atmosphere of prayer and recollection. The gift shop features religious books, cards, icons, crafts, as well as CDs and cassettes of Gregorian chant.

Downside Abbey

Stratton-on-the-Fosse, Bath BA3 4RH
Tel: (01761) 235-100 • Fax: (01761) 235-105, 235-124
Web Site: www.downside.co.uk

Founded in 1854, today Downside Abbey is home to a community of Benedictine monks. As well as touring the vast and beautiful church, visitors can spend time attending religious services with the monks, which includes the singing of the Divine Office and Mass in Gregorian chant. The monastery operates an excellent guesthouse, "The Bainesbury House," which features twenty rooms (sixteen singles, four doubles), a garden, library, restaurant, and several meeting rooms. Classical music concerts, which are open to all visitors, are held throughout the year at the abbey.

Ampleforth Abbey

York, YO6 4EN
Tel: (01439) 766-000, 766-714 • Fax: (01439) 766-724, 788-770
E-mail: monks@ampleforth.org.uk
Web Site: www.ampleforth.org.uk

Founded in 1802, today Ampleforth Abbey is home to a Benedictine community of about one hundred monks. More than ten thousand people visit the monastery annually for a time of recollection and quiet prayer, or to participate in the various retreats and courses offered. Guest rooms are available for those who wish to participate in the monastic life of prayers.

FRANCE

✠

Monastère Notre-Dame-de-la-Paix-Dieu
1064 chemin de Cabanoule
30140 Anduze
Tel: (04) 66-61-73-44 • Fax: (04) 66-61-87-94

Founded in 1970, the Monastery of Notre-Dame-de-la-Paix-Dieu is home to a women's community of Cistercian-Trappist monks. Mass and the Liturgy of the Hours are celebrated daily in French. Both are open to the public. Nine guest rooms are available for those individuals who wish to participate in a personal retreat in a monastic environment.

Monastère de la Théophanie
Monastère Grec Catholique
Le Ladeix
19190 Aubazine
Tel/Fax: (05) 55-25-75-67

Founded in 1965, the Monastery of Théophanie is home to a small monastic community of nuns who belong to the Greek Melkite Catholic Church (a Byzantine Rite church in communion with Rome). Nestled in the foothills of southwestern France, the  monastery's function is to make the richness of Eastern Christian Liturgy and Spirituality known to the western world. Thirteen guest rooms are available for women, priests, religious, couples, and families. Men may be accommodated, but they must present proper references (for example, a letter from their parish priest). The religious services are sung in French, with some traditional Greek and Arabic melodies. For their apostolic ministry, the sisters create incense, translate religious works, make rugs, and perform agricultural duties. Some items available in their gift shop include incense, icons, oriental prayer beads, prayer rugs (pure wool), walnuts, and medicinal herbs. English, French, and Dutch are spoken at the monastery.

Prieuré Sainte–Marie
La Cotellerie
53170 Bazougers
Tel: (02) 4366-43-66 • Fax: (02) 43-66-43-67

Founded in 1971, the Priory of Sainte-Marie is home to a community of Canons Regular. Visitors are invited to participate in the religious services, which includes Mass and the Liturgy of the Hours (both of which are sung in French). A guesthouse for families is available (fifteen rooms), as well as a dormitory for young people. The priory gift shop sells honey, fruits, fresh apple cider, icons, medals, and religious books.

Abbaye Notre–Dame–du–Bec
27800 le Bec-Hellouin
Tel: (02) 32-44-86-09 • Fax: (02) 32-44-96-69

Founded in 1034, the world famous Abbey of Notre-Dame-du-Bec was once home to the great Saint Anselm, and today is home to a community of Benedictine-Olivetan monks. Visitors to the monastery can not only join in the Liturgy of the Hours and Mass of the monks (sung in Gregorian chant and French), but can also take a guided tour of the historic abbey and church. The monastery has two separate guesthouses: one within the abbey complex; the other, on the exterior. Reservations are required at least one month in advance.

Abbaye Notre–Dame–de–Bellefontaine
49122 Bégrolles en Mauges
Tel: (02) 41-75-60-40, 41-75-60-41, 41-75-60-45 • Fax: (02) 41-75-60-49
E-mail: abbaye.bellefontaine@wanadoo.fr
Web Site: www.bellefontaine-abbaye.com

Founded in the eleventh century by the Benedictines, today the Abbey of Notre-Dame-de-Bellefontaine is home to a community of Cistercian-Trappist monks. All religious services are open to the public. The Liturgy of the Hours is sung in French, and parts of the Mass in Gregorian chant. Men and mixed groups can be accommodated for days of prayer and retreat.

Abbaye Sainte-Marie-du-Désert

31530 Bellegarde-Sainte-Marie
Tel: (05) 62-13-45-45 • Fax: (05) 62-13-45-35
E-mail: abstemarie@inTel:com.fr
Web Site: http://www.chez.com/abbayesaintemariedudesert

Founded in 1852, the Abbey of Sainte-Marie-du-Désert is home to a community of Cistercian monks. Offices are sung in French, and all visitors are welcome to join the monks in their daily life of prayer. A guesthouse with twenty-five rooms is available for individuals and small groups seeking a time of prayer and silence. Gift shop items include the abbey's candies, honey, books, and religious objects.

Monastère Notre-Dame-des-Sept-Douleurs

60, avenue Général-Compans
31700 Blagnac
Tel: (05) 34-60-53-90 • Fax: (05) 61-30-46-34

Founded in 1852, today the Monastery of Notre-Dame-des-Sept-Douleurs is home to a women's community of Dominican monks. Mass, Eucharistic Adoration, and other religious services in the chapel are open to the public. A family "pension" connected to the monastery offers comfortable guest rooms for visitors seeking a spiritual retreat. A park and garden are nearby.

Abbaye Notre-Dame-de-Bon-Secours

"La Trappe"
84570 Blauvac
Tel: (04) 90-61-81-17 • Fax: (04) 90-61-98-07

Founded in 1820, Our Lady of Bon Secours Abbey is home to a community of Cistercian-Trappist nuns. Guest rooms are available for those individuals who come for a time of prayer and silence. All visitors are encouraged to join the monks in the Liturgy of the Hours and Mass (sung in both French and Gregorian chant). The abbey gift shop features beehive produce, lavender essence, olive wood crosses, rosaries, and hosts.

Monastère Sainte-Anne
26260 Bonlieu-sur-Roubion
Tel: (04) 75-53-92-23 • Fax: (04) 75-53-86-50

Founded in 1171 by the Cistercians, today the Monastery of Sainte-Anne is home to a community of Premonstratensian Canons Regular (Norbertine Fathers). Visitors are welcome to join the monks in their daily life of prayer in the abbey church. A guesthouse is available, but reservations should be made in advance of your arrival by either sending a fax or a letter to the guestmaster.

Communauté Monastère Notre-Dame
73, route de Mi-Feuillage
45460 Bouzy-la-Foret
Tel (Guesthouse): (02) 38-46-88-99 • Fax: (02) 38-46-88-97
E-mail: ndcalee@aol.com

Founded in 1617, the monastery is home to a community of Benedictine nuns. As well as devoting their lives to prayer, these sisters are best known for their production of Emerald Water. Very rich in essential oils, this lotion has many different uses, but it is especially soothing for minor cuts and burns. In 2000, the sisters moved into a newly constructed monastery, which features a guesthouse of ten rooms. Only priests, religious sisters, couples, and women can be accommodated.

Abbaye Notre-Dame-de-Grâce
50260 Bricquebec
Tel: (02) 33-52-20-01 • Fax: (02) 33-52-56-51
Tel/Fax: (02) 33-52-29-69

Founded in 1824, Our Lady of Grace Abbey is home to a community of Cistercian-Trappist monks. Offices are chanted in French, and all visitors are encouraged to join the monks in prayer. Guest rooms are available only for men (for a maximum of seven days), who must be there for spiritual purposes. You may purchase CDs and cassette recordings of Gregorian chant, as well as liturgical chants in both French and Japanese, at the abbey gift shop.

Abbaye La-Joie-Notre-Dame

56800 Campénéac
Tel: (02) 97-93-42-07 • Fax: (02) 97-93-11-23

Founded in 1921, the Abbey of La-Joie-Notre-Dame is home to a community of Cistercian monks. Guest rooms are available for individuals and groups seeking a place of retreat. All visitors are encouraged to join the monks in their daily life of prayer, which includes Mass and the Liturgy of the Hours. Chocolate, cheese, fruit, and biscuits are just some of the abbey's products that may be purchased in their gift shop.

Abbaye Notre-Dame-de-Lérins

Île Saint-Honorat, B.P. 157
06406 Cannes Cedex
Tel: (04) 92-99-54-00, 92-99-54-10 • Fax: (04) 92-99-54-01, 92-99-54-11
E-mail (Guesthouse): hotellerie@abbayedelerins.com
E-mail (Abbey): info@abbayedelerins.com
Web Site: www.abbayedelerins.com

Founded in 1869, today the Abbey of Notre-Dame-de-Lérins is home to the Congregation of the Immaculate Conception of Sénanque and Lérins. The Offices are sung in French and Byzantine chant, and everyone is invited to join the monks in their life of prayer. Guest rooms are available for those individuals seeking spiritual refreshment and peace. Among the products available for purchase are the abbey's various liqueurs (La Lérina and La Sénancole), wines, and a variety of different kinds of honey.

Communauté des Soeurs Dominicaines de Sainte-Catherine-de-Ricci

16, avenue Isola-Bella
06400 Cannes
Tel: (04) 93-38-06-09 • Fax: (04) 93-39-71-40

Home to a community of contemplative Dominican nuns, the Monastery of Sainte-Catherine-de-Ricci welcomes visitors to their guesthouse for prayer and personal retreats. Twelve guest rooms are available. All individuals are invited to participate in their religious services.

Monastère Notre-Dame-de-l'Action-de-Grâces

10-12, rue Pasteur
11400 Castelnaudary
Tel: (04) 68-23-12-92

Founded in 1854, the Monastery of Notre-Dame-de-l'Action-de-Grâces is home to a community of Poor Clares of Perpetual Adoration. All visitors are welcome to join religious services in the chapel, which includes Mass and the Liturgy of the Hours. A guesthouse, located on the exterior of the monastery, provides accommodation for up to thirty visitors. Guest rooms located within the monastic enclosure are available for consecrated religious and young women who are considering a vocation.

Abbaye Notre-Dame-de-la-Grâce-Dieu

25530 Chaux-les-Passavant
Tel: (03) 81-60-44-45 • Fax: (03) 81-60-44-18

Founded in 1139, the Abbey of Notre-Dame-de-la-Grâce-Dieu is home to a community of Cistercian monks. Visitors are welcome to attend the monks' Mass and Divine Office (held in the abbey chapel), both of which are sung in French and Gregorian chant. In their guesthouse, the monks can receive priests, consecrated religious, women, couples, and young people. All visitors are expected to respect the monastic atmosphere of prayer and silence. A film about the history of the abbey can be viewed upon request.

Carmel
Chavagnes-en-Paillers
85250 Saint-Fulgent
Tel: (02) 5-42-21-80

Founded in 1617, the convent is home to a community of Carmelite monks. Both the Liturgy of the Hours and Mass are open to the public, and everyone is encouraged to participate. Those individuals who wish to pursue a personal retreat in a cloistered environment may request accommodations in their guesthouse. Annually, on the last Sunday in August, there is a great pilgrimage to the convent where celebrations are held in honor of the Blessed Virgin Mary.

Abbaye Saint-Michel-de-Cuxa
66500 Codalet
Tel/Fax: (04) 68-96-02-40

Founded in 878, the Abbey of Saint Michael of Cuxa is home to a community of Benedictine monks. Guided tours of the tenth-century church and crypt are available, and visitors are welcome to attend Mass and Vespers. Guest rooms are available for those who wish to participate in the life of the monks and spend a few days in retreat. Wine, cheese, and ceramics are all available at the abbey gift shop.

Abbaye Sainte-Foy
12320 Conques
Tel: (05) 65-69-85-12 • Fax: (05) 65-72-81-01

Founded in 1120, the Abbey of Sainte-Foy is home to a community of Premonstratensian Canons (Norbertine Fathers). Both the Liturgy of the Hours and Mass are open to the public, and everyone is invited to attend. The abbey operates a guesthouse and dormitory, which provides accommodation for those who seek either a personal or group retreat.

Monastère Sainte-Claire
53, rue des Auberts
26400 Crest
Tel: (04) 75-25-49-13 • Fax: (04) 75-25-28-80

Founded in 1826, the Monastery of Sainte-Claire is home to a community of Poor Clare nuns. Visitors are invited to attend both the Mass and Vespers in the abbey. The monastery provides several types of accommodation, making it suitable for individuals, families, or groups.

Prieuré Notre-Dame-d'Espérance
4, rue Pétrie
Croixault
80290 Poix de Picardie
Tel: (03) 22-90-01-27 • Fax: (03) 22-90-64-33

Founded in 1966, Our Lady of Hope Priory is recognized as the first member of the "Our Lady of Hope" Congregation. All Offices are in French. The priory's guest rooms can accommodate up to thirty people.

Abbaye de Notre-Dame-de-Sept-Fons
03290 Dompierre-sur-Besbre
Tel: (04) 70-48-14-90 • Fax: (04) 70-48-14-93
E-mail: patr.ol@wanadoo.fr
Web Site: www.abbayedeseptfons.com

Founded in 1132, the Abbey of Notre-Dame-de-Sept-Fons is home to a community of Trappist monks. All visitors are invited to attend Mass in the abbey chapel. Those individuals who wish to embark on a monastic retreat of prayer and silence can be accommodated in one of the abbey's twenty-seven guest rooms. An excellent thirty-minute film about the life and history of the abbey is available upon request.

Abbaye Saint-Benoît-d'En-Calcat

81110 Dourgne
Tel: (05) 63-50-84-10 • Fax: (05) 63-50-34-90
E-mail: encalcat.hotellerie@wanadoo.fr

Founded in 1890, the Abbey of Saint-Benoît-d'En-Calcat is home to a community of Benedictine monks. As well as touring the abbey church, visitors can participate in religious services with the monks, which are sung in both French and Gregorian chant. With excellent guesthouse facilities, the abbey provides three types of accommodation: (1) thirty rooms for men inside the monastic enclosure; (2) twenty-three rooms for women or families; (3) two dormitories with twenty-five beds for young people. Among the many items available at the gift shop are the abbey's religious artwork, ceramics, and music tapes and CDs.

Abbaye Sainte-Scholastique

81110 Dourgne
Tel: (05) 63-50-31-32 • Fax: (05) 63-50-12-18
E-mail: sasco81@aol.com

Founded in 1890, the Abbey of Saint Scholastica is home to a community of Benedictine monks. Everyone is encouraged to join the monks in the Liturgy of the Hours and Mass, both of which are sung in French and Gregorian chant. The abbey features two types of accommodation: regular bedrooms for individuals and couples; and dormitory-style rooms for groups of young people. Some of the items that may be purchased at the abbey are ceramics, beehive products, paintings, tapestries, icons, religious books, and stained glass.

Abbaye Notre-Dame-de-Bonne-Espérance

24410 Echourgnac
Tel: (05) 53-80-82-50 • Fax: (05) 53-80-08-36
E-mail: gm.echourgnac@wanadoo.fr

Founded in 1868, the Abbey of Notre-Dame-de-Bonne-Espérance is home to a community of Trappist monks. All visitors are welcome to attend religious services with the monks, which are sung in both French and Gregorian chant. The abbey guesthouse is open (except during the month of January) to all individuals who seek a place of prayer and silence. Since cheese-making is one of the major activities of the monks, visitors may purchase some of these cheeses at the abbey gift shop.

Abbaye Notre-Dame-de-Port-du-Salut

53260 Entrammes
Tel: (02) 43-64-18-64, 43-64-18-60 • Fax: (02) 43-64-18-63

Founded in 1815, Our Lady of Port du Salut Abbey is home to a community of Cistercian-Trappist monks. The offices are chanted in French, with some Latin Gregorian chant. Guest rooms are available to those people who wish to participate in a monastic retreat. All visitors can purchase some of the monastery's homegrown produce at the abbey store.

Abbaye Saint-Joseph-de-Clairval

21150 Flavigny-sur-Ozerain
Tel: (03) 80-96-22-31 • Fax: (03) 80-96-25-29
E-mail: englishspoken@clairval.com
Web Site: www.clairval.com

Founded in 1972, the Benedictine abbey of Saint Joseph of Clairval provides a very authentic monastic experience for all visitors. The Mass and Divine Office are sung in Latin and Gregorian chant, which all are invited to attend. If you are unable to visit the abbey, you can still stay in touch with them by receiving their excellent monthly newsletter which provides inspirational stories providing spiritual comfort and strength. To become a subscriber, simply contact the abbey at the e-mail or mailing address on the previous page and ask to be put on their mailing list. You can purchase Gregorian chant CDs and cassettes, as well as exceptionally beautiful religious images and icons, from the abbey by mail. Men can be accommodated in the monastic guest rooms, but you must write to the guestmaster prior to your visit.

Abbaye Notre-Dame-de-Fontgombault

36220 Fontgombault
Tel: (02) 54-37-12-03 • Fax: (02) 54-37-12-56

Founded in 1091, the Abbey of Notre-Dame-de-Fontgombault is home to a community of Benedictine monks who belong to the Congregation of Solesmes. All visitors are welcome to join the monks in their daily life of prayer, which includes Mass and the singing of the Divine Office in Gregorian chant. Guest rooms are available to those individuals who wish to spend a few days in a monastic atmosphere of prayer and silence. At the gift shop, you may purchase many religious products as well as other items, including the abbey's pottery, farm and garden produce, and their own Gregorian chant CDs and cassettes.

Abbaye Notre-Dame

04310 Ganagobie
Tel: (04) 92-68-00-04 • Fax: (04) 92-68-11-49
E-mail: ste.madeleine@ndganagobie.com
Web Site: www.ndganagobie.com

Founded in 950, today the Monastery of Ganagobie is home to a community of Benedictine monks who belong to the Congregation of Solesmes. Daily Mass and the Liturgy of the Hours are sung in Gregorian chant, and all visitors are welcome to join in the prayer life of the monks. The abbey has fifteen guest rooms for individuals who are seeking a time of retreat and silence. They also have (separate) housing for groups and young people. Jam, honey, perfume, and Gregorian chant CDs are just some of the items available at the abbey gift shop.

Abbaye Sainte-Marie-du-Mont-des-Cats

59270 Godewaersvelde
Tel (Abbey): (03) 28-42-52-50 • Tel (Guesthouse): (03) 28-42-58-22
Fax: (03) 28-42-54-80, 28-49-14, 28-49-49-79, 28-49-48-25
E-mail: montdescats@compuserve.com
abbe@abbaye-montdescats.com
econome@abbaye-montdescats.com
fromagerie@abbaye-montdescats.com
Web Site: www.abbaye-montdescats.com

Founded in 1826, the Abbey of Sainte-Marie-du-Mont-des-Cats is home to a community of Trappist monks. All visitors are invited to attend the religious services, which include both Mass and the Liturgy of the Hours. A guesthouse is available to those individuals who wish to participate in a monastic retreat of prayer and silence. The abbey is very well known for its production of cheese.

Abbaye Notre-Dame-de-Sénanque

84220 Gordes
Tel: (04) 90-72-05-72, 90-72-02-05 • Fax: (04) 90-72-15-70, 90-72-07-45
E-mail: ndsenanque@aol.com
Web Site: www.senanque.fr

Founded in 1148, the Abbey of Notre-Dame-de-Sénanque is home to a community of Cistercian monks. Visitors can participate in the prayer life of the monks by attending their religious services, which are sung in French, Byzantine, and  Gregorian chant. Individuals and groups who wish to embark on a retreat in a traditional monastic environment can ask to be accommodated in one of the abbey's guest rooms. Tours to designated parts of the twelfth-century monastery are available.

Abbaye Notre-Dame de Jouarre

6, rue Montmorin
77640 Jouarre
Tel: (01) 60-22-06-11 • Fax: (01) 60-22-31-25

Founded in 635, Our Lady of Jouarre Abbey is home to the Benedictine community of Mary's Immaculate Heart. Visitors can join the nuns in their life of prayer in the monastery church (offices are sung in French and Gregorian chant), as well as take a guided tour of the seventh-century crypt. Guest rooms are available for families, young people, individuals, and groups. Some of the craft items that may be purchased include the abbey's ceramics, pottery, small statues, and nativity scenes.

Abbaye Saint-Martin de Mondaye

14250 Juaye-Mondaye
Tel: (02) 31-92-58-11 • Fax: (02) 31-92-08-05
Web Site: www.mondaye.com

Founded in the thirteenth century, the Abbey of Saint-Martin de Monday is home to a community of Premonstratensian Canons (Norbertine Fathers). As well as taking guided tours of the abbey, visitors can attend daily religious services with the monks. Those individuals or groups who wish to spend several days at the abbey in spiritual retreat should contact the guestmaster prior to their arrival.

Abbaye Saint-Guénolé

29560 Landévennec
Tel: (02) 98-27-73-34 • Fax: (02) 98-27-79-57
Tel (Guesthouse): (02) 98-27-37-53
E-mail: abbaye.landevennec@wanadoo.fr

Founded in the sixth century, the Abbey of Saint-Guénolé is home to a Benedictine community of monks who belong to the Congregation of Subiaco. Offices are chanted in French, with some pieces in Gregorian chant. Guest rooms are available, on a limited basis, to those who wish to participate in the prayer life of the monks. Fruit preserves, ceramics, and music cassettes are just some of the articles available at the abbey gift shop.

Abbaye de La Coudre

Rue Saint-Benoît
53005 Laval
Tel: (02) 43-02-85-85 • Fax: (02) 43-66-90-18
E-mail: abbcoudre@aol.com

Founded in 1816, the Abbey of La Coudre is home to a community of Cistercian-Trappist monks. Visitors can participate in religious services, which are sung in both French and Gregorian chant. Guest rooms are available to those individuals who wish to participate in a monastic retreat. Well known for its cheese and dairy products, they are sold by the abbey throughout France and Belgium.

Abbaye Sainte–Madeleine

84330 Le Barroux
Tel: (04) 90-62-56-05

Founded in 1970, the Abbey of Saint Magdalene offers a very authentic experience of traditional monasticism. Guests can participate in the Divine Office and Mass, which are celebrated in the Traditional Latin Rite and sung in Gregorian chant. Guest rooms are only available to men and young people who are seeking a quiet time of prayer and seclusion. Please contact the guestmaster before planning to stay overnight in the monastery since space is limited. Some of the items that may be purchased are the abbey's CDs and cassettes, as well as their special bread and shortbread biscuits. Less than two miles from the monastery is the Abbey of Notre-Dame-de-l'Annonciation (see following entry).

Abbaye de Notre–Dame–de–l'Annonciation

La Font de Pertus
84330 Le Barroux
Tel: (04) 90-65-29-29 • Fax: (04) 90-65-29-30

Founded in 1979, the Abbey of Notre-Dame-de-l'Annonciation is home to a community of Benedictine nuns. Visitors are welcome to all the Offices as well as the daily Latin Tridentine Mass which are sung in Latin and Gregorian chant. The abbey gift shop is open throughout the year, except during its annual retreat (usually in May). Some of the many items that may be purchased are icons, candies, postcards, paintings, jam (made by the sisters with the apricots from their orchard), and recordings of Gregorian chant sung by the nuns in the monastery. Since they have no apostolic duties, the sisters devote themselves to a life of prayer, study, and work. French, English, German, Polish, and Spanish are all spoken at the abbey. A guesthouse has not yet been opened to the public.

Communauté de l'Abbaye
B.P. 3
50170 Le Mont-Saint-Michel
Tel: (02) 33-60-14-47 • Fax: (02) 33-60-31-02
E-mail: abbayemichel@wanadoo.fr

Founded in the tenth century, the Abbey of Mont-Saint-Michel is an architectural and artistic wonder. To this day, it remains one of the most famous monasteries in all Christendom. Throughout the year, guided tours of the abbey are available (in various languages including English) which provide an insider's glimpse into Medieval Europe. Home to a Benedictine Diocesan community since 1969, the monastery offers a limited number of guest rooms to those visitors who are seeking a place of Catholic worship, prayer, and retreat. Reservations must be made well in advance.

Abbaye Notre-Dame-des-Dombes
01330 Le Plantay
Tel: (04) 74-98-14-40 • Fax: (04) 74-98-16-70
E-mail: dombes.abi@wanadoo.fr

Founded in 1863, the Abbey of Notre-Dame-des-Dombes is home to a community of Trappist monks. A hostel is available to those individuals who wish to participate in a personal retreat, and join the monks in the prayer life of their community. The Liturgy of the Hours and Mass are sung in French. Among the many items available at the gift shop are the abbey's fruit preserves.

Prieuré Saint–Benoît–de–Chauveroche
90200 Lepuix-Gy
Tel: (03) 84-29-01-57 • Fax: (03) 84-29-56-80

Founded in 1980, the Priory of Saint-Benoît-de-Chauveroche is home to a community of Benedictine monks. All Offices are chanted in French, which everyone is invited to attend. A small guesthouse of seven rooms is available to individuals who want to participate more fully in the prayer life of the community. There is also another guesthouse located not far from the priory which has six rooms and twenty-five beds.

Abbaye Saint–Martin
2 Place Lambert
86240 Ligugé
Tel: (05) 49-55-21-12 • Fax: (05) 49-55-10-98
E-mail: info@abbaye-liguge.com
Web Site: www.abbaye-liguge.com

Founded in 361, today the Abbey of Saint Martin is home to a community of Benedictine monks who belong to the Congregation of Solesmes. Visitors are welcome to join the monks in their daily life of prayer, which includes singing the Divine Office and Mass in Gregorian chant. The abbey offers several different types of guesthousing, each one catering to men, women, young people, and groups. Gregorian chant CDs and cassettes are available at the gift shop, as well as many other  religious items including stained-glass creations and reproductions.

Abbaye Notre-Dame de Melleray

La Melleraye de Bretagne
44520 Moisdon La Rivière
Tel: (02) 40-55-20-01

Founded in 1142, Our Lady of Melleray Abbey is home to a community of Cistercian-Trappist monks. Guest rooms are available for retreat participants, and all visitors are encouraged to join the monks in the Liturgy of the Hours (which is sung in French). The abbey features a bookstore and has a number of craft items for sale, including religious graphic arts.

Abbaye Notre-Dame-d'Aiguebelle

26230 Montjoyer
Tel: (04) 75-98-64-70, 75-98-64-78 • Fax: (04) 75-98-64-71, 75-98-64-79
E-mail: ab.aiguebelles@wanadoo.fr
Web Site: www.abbaye-aiguebelle.com

Founded in 1137, the Abbey of Notre-Dame-d'Aiguebelle is home to a Cistercian-Trappist community of monks. All visitors are welcome to join the monks in the Liturgy of the Hours and Mass, which are sung in French, Byzantine and Latin Gregorian chant. A guesthouse with fifty rooms is available to those individuals seeking a place of prayer and silence. Reservations are required. Many of the abbey's products are available in the gift shop, including a selection of their syrups, honey, and liqueurs.

Prieuré Saint-Dodon

18, Grand-rue
59132 Moustier-en-Fagne
Tel: (03) 27-61-81-28 • Fax: (03) 27-61-81-12

Founded in 1968, the Priory of Saint-Dodon is home to a community of Benedictine monks. Visitors are invited to participate in the religious services, which are said in the Byzantine Rite. A few guest rooms are available for priests, consecrated religious, and laypeople who are seeking a time of prayer and solitude.

Monastère de la Visitation
192, rue Lorthiois
59420 Mouvaux
Tel: (03) 20-26-94-34

Founded in 1876, the Monastery of the Visitation is home to a community of Visitation monks. The abbey chapel is open throughout the day, all religious services are open to the public (they are said/sung in French). Individuals or small groups who want to participate more fully in the prayer life of the monks may be accommodated in their guesthouse. Only young women and consecrated religious, however, can ask to be accommodated in the guest rooms within the monastic enclosure.

Monastère de la Visitation
49, route des Saulaies
58000 Nevers
Tel: (03) 86-57-37-40 • Fax: (03) 86-57-25-98

Founded in 1616, the Monastery of the Visitation is home to a community of Visitation monks. All are welcome to participate in the religious services of the abbey, which includes Mass and the Liturgy of the Hours. Nine guest rooms are available to those individuals who want to participate in a monastic retreat of prayer and silence. The monastery is located in the same town as the shrine and convent of Saint Gildard, which houses the incorrupt body of Saint Bernadette Soubirous (the visionary child from Lourdes).

Prieuré Saint-Benoît-Sainte-Scholastique
3, cité du Sacré-Coeur
75018 Paris
Tel: (0146) 06-14-74 • Fax: (0142) 23-19-33

Founded in 1898, the Priory of Saint-Benoît-Sainte-Scholastique is home to a community of Benedictine monks of Sacré-Cœur-de-Montmarte. All religious services are open to the public, and are chanted in French. Individuals, groups, and pilgrims are all welcome to spend several days in retreat at the abbey guesthouse. The monastery is located near the world famous Basilica of Sacré-Coeur.

Monastère de Marie, Mère de Miséricorde

3, rue Notre-Dame
36180 Pellevoisin
Tel/Fax: (02) 54-39-0-91

Founded in 1893, the Monastery of Marie, Mère de Miséricorde (Mary, Mother of Mercy) is home to a community of Dominican monks who serve as custodians of the Shrine of Our Lady of Pellevoisin. The Liturgy of the Hours and Mass are chanted in French and are open to the public. With only seven guest rooms available, individuals must come with a desire to participate in the prayer life of the monastery. To learn more about the shrine and the Church-approved apparitions of the Virgin Mary that took place here in the eighteenth century, please refer to my book *Catholic Shrines of Western Europe: A Pilgrim's Travel Guide* (published by Liguori Publications).

Abbaye Notre-Dame de Tamié

Col de Tamié
73200 Tamié (Plancherine)
Tel: (04) 79-31-15-50 • Fax: (04) 79-37-05-24
E-mail: tamie.abbaye@wanadoo.fr
Web Site: www.abbaye-tamie.com

Founded in 1132, Our Lady of Tamié Abbey is home to a community of Cistercian-Trappist monks. Guest rooms are available to both men and women who wish to spend up to seven days in silence and prayer. Among the many products available at the gift shop is the abbey's famous Tamié cheese.

Abbaye Sainte-Anne-de-Kergonan
B.P. 11
56340 Plouharnel
Tel: (02) 97-52-30-75 • Fax: (02) 97-52-41-20

Founded in 1897, the Abbey of Sainte-Anne-de-Kergonan is home to a community of Benedictine monks who belong to the Congregation of Solesmes. Fifteen guest rooms are available to men who wish to participate in the monastic life of the abbey for a few days. All Offices and the Mass are sung in Gregorian chant, which all visitors are welcome to attend. Pottery, ceramics, videocassettes, and Gregorian chant CDs are just some of the items available at the abbey gift shop.

Monastère de Sainte-Claire
13, rue Sainte-Colette
39800 Poligny
Tel: (03) 84-37-11-40 • Fax: (03) 84-37-07-53

Founded in 1783, the Monastery of Sainte-Claire is home to a community of Poor Clare nuns. Serving both as an abbey and a shrine, pilgrims can come here and pray before the tomb of Saint Colette. As well as attending religious services with the nuns, visitors can join in the many celebrations that take place throughout the year in honor of Saint Colette. The most popular day of pilgrimage takes place on March 6, the feast day of Saint Colette. The monastery features eight guest rooms, with preference given to visiting priests and sisters.

Abbaye Saint Joseph and Saint Peter of Pradines
42630 Pradines
Tel: (04) 77-64-80-06 • Fax: (04) 77-64-82-08

Founded in 1818, the Abbey of Saint Joseph and Saint Peter of Pradines is home to the Benedictine community of Mary's Immaculate Heart. All are welcome to join the nuns in their daily life of prayer. Those who want to spend quiet time in retreat can inquire about staying in one of their guest rooms. The abbey's gift shop features its own woven items, silk scarves, as well as other craft items.

Abbaye Notre-Dame-de-Timadeuc
B.P. 17
Bréhan
56580 Rohan
Tel: (02) 97-51-50-29 • Fax: (02) 97-51-59-20
E-mail: timadeuc.abbaye@wanadoo.fr

Founded in 1841, Our Lady of Timadeuc Abbey is home to a community of Cistercian-Trappist monks. The Liturgy of the Hours is chanted in French, with some Gregorian chant. With more than forty guest rooms available, both men and women are welcome  to stay at the monastery for times of prayer and reflection. Two large dormitory-style rooms with twenty-eight beds are available to groups of young people. Among the most popular items that visitors can purchase at the gift shop are the abbey's fruit preserves, cheese, religious icons, CDs, and cassettes.

Monastère des Bénédictines du Saint-Sacrement

1, rue Saint-Benoît
67560 Rosheim
Tel: (03) 88-50-41-67 • Fax: (03) 88-50-42-71
E-mail: benedictines@media-net.fr
Web Site: www.benedictines-rosheim.com

Founded in 1862, the Monastery of Saint-Sacrement is home to a community of Benedictine monks. Visitors are invited to attend religious services which are sung in Gregorian chant. The abbey operates a guesthouse which is available to individuals, couples, families, and groups. Private lessons and classes to learn Gregorian chant are available. One of the major duties of the monks is the making of hosts.

Abbaye de Chambarand

La Trappe
38940 Roybon
Tel: (04) 76-36-22-68 • Fax: (04) 76-36-28-65
E-mail: ab.chambarand@wanadoo.fr,
la.trappe@wanadoo.fr
Web Site: www.chambarand.com

Founded in 1931, the Abbey of Chambarand is home to a community of Cistercian-Trappist monks. Mass is celebrated daily in the chapel, with vespers in the evening (both are sung in French and Gregorian chant). The guesthouse is reserved solely for retreat participants and the families of the monks. The abbey is very renowned for their production of various cheeses, butter, and other dairy products.

Abbaye de Fleury

45730 Saint-Benoît-sur-Loire
Tel: (02) 38-35-72-43 • Fax: (02) 38-35-77-82, 38-35-77-71
Web Sites: www.abbaye-fleury.com
www.abbaye.chez.tiscali.fr

Dating back to the seventh century, the Abbey of Saint Fleury is not only home to a community of Benedictine monks who belong to the Congregation of Subiaco, but is also home to the sacred remains of Saint Benedict —the founder of western monasticism. Each year, thousands of pilgrims and visitors come to pray at his tomb, and experience the tranquillity of monastic life. Guest accommodations are available to those who wish to join the monks in their daily life of prayer, and spend time in a personal or group retreat. Offices are sung in French and Latin, with Gregorian chant at Mass.

Monastère Notre-Dame-des-Petites-Roches

38660 Saint Bernard du Touvet
Tel: (04) 76-08-31-13 • Fax: (04) 76-08-32-17

Founded in 1970, the monastery of Notre-Dame-des-Petites-Roches is home to a community of Cistercian monks. All visitors are invited to attend religious services, which include the Liturgy of the Hours and Mass (both of which are sung in French). A guesthouse is available to those individuals or groups who wish to participate in the prayer life of the monks.

Monastère de la Visitation

7, av. du Docteur-Mallet
15100 Saint-Flour
Tel: (04) 71-60-07-82 • Fax: (04) 71-60-43-97

Founded in 1839, the Monastery of the Visitation is home to a community of Carmelite monks. All religious services, which are sung or said in French, are open to the public. Guest rooms are limited to those individuals seeking a cloistered environment of prayer and silence.

Abbaye Notre-Dame-des-Gardes

49120 Saint-Georges-des-Gardes
Tel: (02) 41-29-57-10 • Fax: (02) 41-29-57-19

Founded in 1818, the Abbey of Notre-Dame-des-Gardes is home to a community of Trappist monks. All visitors are invited to participate in the prayer life of the monks, which includes Mass and the Liturgy of the Hours (sung in French). The guesthouse is available to women, couples, consecrated religious, young people, as well as groups of both men and women for times of personal retreat. Some of the monks' "homemade" products can be purchased at the monastery.

Prieuré Saint-Jacques

50240 Saint-James
Tel: (02) 33-48-31-39 • Fax: (02) 33-48-67-23

Founded in 1930, the Priory of Saint-Jacques is home to a community of Benedictine monks of Jesus Crucified. All visitors are welcome to attend religious services with the monks, including Mass and the Liturgy of the Hours (sung in French). Those individuals and groups who wish to participate more fully in the prayer life of the monks may ask to be accommodated in the guesthouse.

Prieuré Notre-Dame-du-Calvaire

86800 Saint-Julien-l'Ars
Tel: (05) 49-56-71-01

Founded in 1617, Our Lady of Calvary Priory is home to a community of Benedictine Nuns. The Offices and Mass are sung in French and Gregorian chant, all visitors are welcome to join the sisters in religious services. Guest rooms are available for both individuals and small groups.

Abbaye de Notre-Dame-des-Neiges

07590 Saint-Laurent-les-Bains
Tel: (04) 66-46-59-00, (04) 66-46-00-38
Fax: (04) 66-46-05-31, (04) 66-46-59-10
Web Site: www.notredamedesneiges.com

Founded in 1850, the Abbey of Notre-Dame-des-Neiges is home to a community of Cistercian monks. All visitors are invited to attend the solemn High Mass with the monks, as well as the Liturgy of the Hours, both of which are celebrated every day. A guesthouse is available to those individuals and groups who wish to participate in a monastic retreat of prayer and silence.

Abbaye Sainte-Marie-de-la-Pierre-qui-Vire

89630 Saint-Léger-Vauban
Tel: (03) 86-33-19-28, 86-33-19-20 • Fax: (03) 86-32-22-33
Web Site: www.abbaye-pierrequivire.asso.fr

Founded in 1850, the Abbey of Sainte-Marie-de-la-Pierre-qui-Vire is home to a community of about seventy Benedictine monks, which belongs to the Congregation of Subiaco. Both the Mass and the Liturgy of the Hours are sung in French and Gregorian chant, which all visitors are invited to attend. The monks operate a guesthouse that is open to those men and women who are seeking a place of spiritual refreshment in a monastic environ-

ment (it is closed in January). Languages spoken at the abbey include French, English, German, Italian, Spanish, and Swedish.

Abbaye de Notre-Dame-de-Cîteaux

21700 Saint-Nicolas-les-Cîteaux
Tel: (03) 80-61-11-53 • Fax: (03) 80-62-36-79
E-mail (community): ab.citeaux@wanadoo.fr
E-mail (tourist information): citeaux.visites@wanadoo.fr
Web Site: www.citeaux-abbaye.com
http://perso.wanadoo.fr/citeaux/etoile.htm

Founded in 1098, the world renowned Abbey of Notre-Dame-de-Cîteaux is home to a community of Cistercian-Trappist monks. The Liturgy of the Hours is sung in French, with parts of the Mass and the evening's *Salve Regina* sung in Gregorian chant. Guest rooms are available to those who wish to join in the prayer life of the monks, and spend quiet time in reflection. Some of the many items you may purchase include the abbey's cheeses, honey, candy, pottery, CDs, and tape cassettes (which are recorded within the monastery).

Abbaye Notre-Dame-de-Belval

Troisvaux
62130 Saint-Pol-sur-Ternoise
Tel: (03) 21-03-11-65, (03) 21-04-10-10 • Fax: (03) 21-47-18-15
E-mail: ab@abbaye-belval.com
celleriere@abbaye-belval.com
Web Site: www.abbaye-belval.com
http://perso.wanadoo.fr/belval

Founded in 1893, the Abbey of Notre-Dame-de-Belval is home to a community of Trappist monks. A guesthouse is available solely for those individuals who want to embark on a spiritual retreat in a monastic environment of prayer and silence. All religious services are sung in French.

Monastère des Bénédictines

51220 Saint-Thierry
Tel: (03) 26-03-10-72 • Fax: (03) 26-03-15-49
Tel/Fax: (03) 26-03-99-37

Originally founded in the fifth century, today the monastery is home to a women's community of Benedictine monks. As well as spending time in the ancient chapel, visitors can attend religious services, which includes Mass and the Divine Office. A guesthouse is available to those individuals who wish to participate more fully in the life of the community, as well as embark on a personal spiritual retreat.

Abbaye Saint–Wandrille

76490 Saint-Wandrille-Rançon
Tel: (02) 35-96-23-11 • Fax: (02) 35-96-49-08
E-mail: abbaye.st-wandrille@wanadoo.fr
Web Site: www.st-wandrille.com

Originally founded in 649, today the Abbey of Saint Wandrille is home to a community of Benedictine monks who belong to the Congregation of Solesmes. Visitors are welcome to join the monks in their daily life of prayer, which includes the singing of the Liturgy of the Hours and Mass in Gregorian chant. Guided tours of the monastery are also available. Guest rooms are available for men at the abbey, while the Saint Joseph House provides accommodation for women and couples. Among the most popular items available at the abbey gift shop are their Gregorian chant CDs and cassette recordings.

Monastère de la Nativité

105, rue Victor-Guichard
89100 Sens
Tel: (03) 86-65-13-41 • Fax: (03) 86-65-73-49

Founded in 1920, the Monastery of the Nativity is home to a community of Dominican monks. As well as attending religious services, visitors can spend time in the crypt praying before the fifteenth-century miraculous statue of Our Lady of Graces. A guesthouse is available to those individuals and groups who are seeking a few days of prayer and reflection. Among the most popular products at the gift shop are the abbey's chocolates.

Abbaye Sainte-Lioba

Quartier Saint-Germain
13109 Simiane-Collongue
Tel: (04) 42-22-60-60 • Fax: (04) 42-22-79-50
E-mail: benedictins@lioba.com
Web Site: www.lioba.com

Founded in 1987, the Abbey of Sainte-Lioba is home to a community of Benedictine monks and nuns. Visitors are welcome to participate in the prayer life of the community, which includes both their Mass and the Liturgy of the Hours (sung in French and Gregorian chant). A guesthouse is available to those individuals seeking spiritual refreshment and solitude in a monastic environment.

Abbaye Saint–Pierre de Solesmes

72300 Solesmes
Tel: (0243) 95-03-08 • Fax: (0243) 95-68-79
E-mail: abbaye@solesmes.com
Web Site: www.solesmes.com

Refounded by Dom Guéranger in 1837, the renowned Abbey of Saint Peter today serves as a worldwide center for Gregorian chant and spirituality. Home to a community of almost ninety Benedictine monks, the abbey has gained international recognition for their recordings and publications of Gregorian chant. All visitors are welcome to join the monks in their daily life of prayer, which includes the singing of the Divine Office and Mass in Latin Gregorian chant. Guest rooms, located within the monastic enclosure, are available to those men who seek a place of retreat and prayer. Guesthouse accommodation, however, is available to both men and women at the monastic hotel *Villa Sainte-Anne*, which is located just two blocks from the Abbey of Saint Peter and operated by the Abbey of Saint Cecilia. All of Solesmes's Gregorian chant recordings (on CD or cassette) can be purchased at the abbey gift shop, as well as throughout the world at many Catholic and secular book and music stores.

Abbaye Sainte–Cécile

Monastic Hotel: Villa Sainte-Anne
21, rue J-Alain
72300 Solesmes
Tel: (0243) 95-45-05

Founded in the nineteenth century, the Abbey of Saint Cecilia is home to a community of about thirty-five Benedictine nuns who belong to the Congregation of Solesmes. Located just two blocks from the renowned Abbey of Saint Peter, the Abbey of Saint Cecilia also serves as a spiritual treasurehouse of Gregorian chant. It has gained worldwide recognition for its recordings of Gregorian chant. Each day offers a full schedule of religious services, including the Divine Office and Mass that is sung in Latin Gregorian chant, which all are invited to attend. Guesthouse accommodation is available to both men and women at the Villa Sainte-Anne monastic hotel. All of Solesmes's Gregorian chant recordings (on CD or cassette) can be purchased at the abbey gift shop, as well as at many Catholic and secular book and music stores throughout the world.

Abbaye La Trappe

61380 Soligny-La-Trappe
Tel: (02) 33-84-17-00, 33-84-17-01 • Fax: (02) 33-34-98-57, 33-84-17-08
E-mail (community): la.trappe@wanadoo.fr

A world-famous monastery, the Abbey of La Trappe is home to a community of Cistercian-Trappist monks who started the Cistercian Reform movement in the early nineteenth century. Only men (individually or in groups) can be accommodated in the monastic guesthouses. All visitors, however, are warmly invited to participate in Mass and Vespers. You can purchase some of the abbey's products, including yogurt, cheese, milk, cream, milk-based desserts, and fruit preserves.

Monastère de la Visitation

Domaine de Guerre
84700 Sorgues
Tel: (04) 90-83-31-14

Founded in 1624, the monastery is home to a community of Visitation monks. All religious services are open to the public, and are sung in French. Seventeen guest rooms are available to those individuals who are seeking a time of prayer and quiet. Many pilgrims come to pray before the tomb of Saint Maxima, a young girl who died as a martyr during the reign of Diocletian.

Abbaye Saint–Michel–de–Frigolet

13150 Tarascon-sur-Rhône
Tel: (04) 90-95-70-07 • Tel (Guesthouse): (04) 90-90-52-70
Fax: (04) 90-95-75-22
E-mail: abbayedefrigolet@frigolet.com
Web Site: www.frigolet.com

Founded in 1133, the Abbey of Saint-Michel-de-Frigolet is home to a community of Premonstratensian Canons (Norbertine Fathers). As well as taking guided tours of the thirteenth-century cloister, Saint Michael Church, and Our Lady of Good Remedy Chapel, visitors can attend religious services. The monastery guesthouse provides accommodation to both men and women who wish to participate in a personal retreat at the abbey. Great celebrations take place at the monastery on the feast day of Our Lady of Good Remedy, which is the first Sunday after May 15. An excellent gift shop can be found on the premises.

Ordre de la Vierge Marie

38, rue J-F Marmontel
94320 Thiais
Tel: (01) 48-84-75-58

Founded in 1501, the monastery is home to members of the Order of the Virgin Mary. All are invited to attend the religious services of the community. A guesthouse with twenty rooms is available to those individuals who are seeking a time of prayer and reflection.

Abbaye Notre–Dame de Tournay

65910 Tournay
Tel: (05) 62-35-70-21

Founded in 1935, the Abbey of Notre-Dame de Tournay is home to a community of Benedictine monks who belong to the Congregation of Subiaco. Visitors are welcome to join the monks in their prayer life, which includes daily recitation of the Liturgy of the Hours and celebration of Mass (both are said in French). Those who desire to participate more fully in the prayer life of the monastery may be accommodated in one of the abbey's guest rooms (thirty rooms for men, twelve for women). Ceramics, candies, fruits, and religious books are just a few of the items available in the abbey gift shop.

Abbaye Notre-Dame-de-Saint-Joseph

88130 Ubexy
Tel: (03) 29-38-04-32 • Fax: (03) 29-38-05-90
E-mail: abbaye.ubexy@wanadoo.fr

Founded in 1841, the Abbey of Notre-Dame-de-Saint-Joseph is home to a community of Cistercians monks. All visitors are invited to attend religious services, which include Mass and Vespers. Both individuals and groups who wish to participate more fully in the prayer life of the monks can be accepted into the guesthouse.

Abbaye Notre-Dame-de-Belloc

64240 Urt
Tel: (05) 59-29-65-55 • Fax: (05) 59-29-44-08
Web Site: www.belloc-urt.org

Founded in 1875, the Abbey of Notre-Dame-de-Belloc is home to a community of Benedictine monks who belong to the Congregation of Subiaco. Daily Offices are sung in French and Latin, with Mass in Gregorian chant. All visitors are invited to participate in the prayer life of the monks, while those individuals and groups desiring a deeper experience of monastic life may be accommodated in the abbey guesthouse. A gift shop on the premises sells the monastery's cheese.

Abbaye Notre-Dame-du-Pré

76540 Valmont
Tel: (02) 35-27-34-92 • Fax: (02) 35-27-86-21

Founded in 1011, the Abbey of Notre-Dame-du-Pré is home to a women's community of Benedictine monks. All visitors are invited to participate in religious services, which include the celebration of Mass and the Divine Office, said/sung in French and Gregorian chant. The monastery guesthouse is open to both individuals and groups who seek a place of prayer and solitude.

Abbaye Saint-Louis-du-Temple
Limon
91430 Vauhallan (Essone)
Tel (Abbey): (01) 69-85-21-00 • Tel (Guesthouse): (01) 69-85-21-20

Founded in 1789, the Abbey of Saint-Louis-du-Temple is home to a community of Benedictine monks. As well as touring the abbey museum and grounds, visitors can attend religious services, which are sung in both French and Gregorian chant. With excellent guesthouse facilities, the abbey has thirty rooms, several meeting rooms, and a small library. Many of the abbey's farm products are available at the gift shop.

Abbaye Saint-Nicolas
124, rue de la Place-Notre-Dame
B.P. 236
27132 Verneuil-sur-Avre
Tel: (02) 32-32-02-94 • Fax: (02) 32-32-72-46

Founded in 1627, the abbey of Saint-Nicolas is home to a community of Benedictine monks. As well as touring the fifteenth-century Gothic church, visitors can join the monks in their celebration of Mass and the Divine Office (which are both sung in Gregorian chant according to the Order of Solesmes).

Association Jérusalem Vezelay
Presbytère
89450 Vézelay
Tel: (03) 86-33-39-50 • Fax: (03) 86-33-36-93

Founded in 1975, the monastery is home to the Monastic Fraternity of Jerusalem. As well as praying before the relics of Saint Mary Magdalene in the crypt of the abbey basilica, visitors can attend religious services with the monks, which are sung in polyphony and French. The monks operate two guesthouses, one of which provides accommodation for twenty people (*Béthanie des Fraternités*), and the other which accommodates up to thirty-five people (*Centre Pax Christi*). Many of the abbey's products and artworks are available in the gift shop (which is located at 78, rue Saint-Pierre).

Monastère de la Visitation
Montée de l'Uriol
38450 Vif
Tel: (04) 76-72-51-18

Founded in 1645, the monastery is home to a community of Visitation monks. Every day, visitors are welcome to join the monks in the abbey chapel for Mass and the Liturgy of the Hours, which are both sung in French. A guesthouse with thirty-five rooms provides accommodation to both men and women, individuals and groups.

Abbaye Notre-Dame-d'Acey
39350 Vitreux
Tel: (03) 84-81-04-11 • Fax: (03) 84-70-90-97

Founded in 1136, the Abbey of Notre-Dame-d'Acey is home to a community of Cistercian-Trappist monks. The abbey church, built in the twelfth century, is a historical monument. Fifteen guest rooms are available to individuals and couples, and the abbey's dormitory can accommodate up to fifty-two people. The abbey operates a factory that works with silver and gold.

Monastère du Chalais
B.P. 128 Chalais
38340 Voreppe
Tel: (04) 76-50-02-16 • Fax: (04) 76-50-22-23

Originally founded at the end of the sixteenth century, today the Monastery of Chalais is home to community of Dominican nuns. As well as spending time in the chapel, visitors can join the sisters in religious services. Thirty guest rooms are available to any individual who seeks a place of prayer and solitude.

Abbaye Saint-Paul

62219 Wisques
Tel: (03) 21-95-11-04, 21-12-28-78, 21-12-28-50
Fax: (03) 21-38-19-40, 21-12-28-79, 21-12-28-51
E-mail: info@abbaye-wisques.com
Web Site: www.abbaye-wisques.com

Founded in 1889, the Abbey of Saint-Paul is home to a community of Benedictine monks which belongs to the Congregation of Solesmes. Visitors are welcome to join the monks in their daily life of prayer, which includes the singing of the Divine Office and Mass in Gregorian chant. The abbey's guesthouse has twenty-eight rooms open to both individuals and groups. The abbey gift shop sells a number of religious art ceramics, as well as Gregorian chant CDs.

Abtei Sankt Erentraud

Kellenried 3
88276 Berg (Ravensburg)
Tel: (07505) 956-60 • Tel (Guesthouse): (07505) 1261
Fax: (07505) 1260

Founded in the eighteenth century, the Abbey of Sankt Erentraud is home to a community of Benedictine monks. Visitors can tour the abbey church (which was restored after World War II) and attend religious services with the monks. Both the Liturgy of the Hours and Mass are sung in Latin and German. Since 1962, the monks have operated a guesthouse which provides accommodation for those individuals who wish to participate in the prayer life of the monks.

Benediktinerabtei Ettal

Kaiser-Ludwig-Platz 1
82488 Ettal
Tel: (08822) 740 • Fax: (08822) 74-228
Fax (Guesthouse): (08822) 74-480
E-mail: hotel@kloster-ettal.de
verwaltung@kloster-ettal.de
Web Site: www.kloster-ettal.de

Founded in 1330, today the Abbey of Ettal is home to a community of Benedictine monks. A place of pilgrimage for many centuries, the monastery still remains one of the most famous abbeys in Germany to this day which is known for its history, architecture, and art. Visitors can participate in the prayer life of the monks by attending Mass and the Divine Office, as well as taking guided tours of the abbey. Guests can stay at the *Ludwig der Bayer Hotel*, which has very comfortable rooms. The hotel also has a number of modern facilities including an indoor pool, sauna, tennis courts, and a restaurant featuring the region's finest cuisine. The abbey produces its own beer which visitors can purchase.

Benediktinermissionare

Kloster Jakobsberg
55435 Gau-Algesheim
Tel: (06725) 304-0, 304-111 • Fax: (06725) 304-100
E-mail: mail@klosterjakobsberg.de
herrmann@klosterjakobsberg.de
Web Site: www.klosterjakobsberg.de

Founded in 1720, the Abbey of Jakobsberg is home to a community of Benedictine monks. Mass and the Liturgy of the Hours are celebrated daily in the abbey church, which all visitors are welcome to attend. Guest rooms are available, but you must come with the intention of participating in the prayer life and work of the monastery. The two major feast days at the abbey are those dedicated to Saint Christopher (July 25) and Saint Barbara (December 4).

Kloster Mariental

65366 Geisenheim (Mayence)
Tel: (06722) 99-580 • Fax: (06722) 99-5813
E-mail: marienthal@franziskaner.de

Founded in 1309, the Cloister of Mariental is home to a community of Franciscan priests and brothers. Visitors can join the Franciscans in Mass and the Liturgy of the Hours, as well as spend time in the Room of Meditation—which lies inside the monastery. Guesthouse accommodations are available for those individuals who wish to join the community in their prayers, work, and meditation (guesthouse visitors must be at least eighteen years of age).

Abtei Oberschönenfeld

86459 Gessertshausen (Augsburg)
Tel: (08238) 962-50 • Fax: (08238) 600-65
E-mail: abtei_oberschoenenfeld@t-online.de

Founded in 1211, the Abbey of Oberschönenfeld is home to a community of Cistercian monks. Religious services are open to the public and are sung in Gregorian chant. The abbey operates a guesthouse which provides comfortable rooms to individuals who wish to participate in a personal retreat in a monastic environment. Some of the monks' artistic works, which are available for purchase, include handcrafted furniture, wooden statues, candles, and embroidered items.

Abtei Himmerod

54534 Grosslittgen (Koblenz)
Tel (Abbey): (06575) 9513-0 • Tel (Guesthouse): (06575) 9513-17
Fax: (06575) 9513-39

Founded in 1134, the Abbey of Himmerod is home to a community of Cistercian monks. Every day, the monks celebrate Mass and the Divine Office in the abbey church. The monastery's very comfortable guesthouse provides accommodation only for men—both individuals and groups are welcome.

Abtei Neuburg

Stiftweg 2
69118 Heidelberg
Tel: (06221) 895-0 • Fax: (06221) 895-166

Founded in 1130, the Abbey of Neuburg is home to a community of Benedictine monks. As well as touring the eighteenth-century abbey church, visitors can stroll in the monastery's grand garden. Mass is celebrated daily, and the two major feast days of Saint Benedict (March 21 and July 11) bring a large number of pilgrims. The abbey operates a simple and peaceful guesthouse, which is open to both men and women who seek a spiritual retreat. The monks produce excellent jams, which are available for visitors and tourists to purchase.

Abtei Mariawald

Gästehaus
52396 Heimbach/Eifel
Tel: (02446) 95-06-0 • Fax: (02446) 95-06-30

Founded in 1470, the Abbey of Mariawald is home to a community of Cistercian monks. Visitors are welcome to join the monks in religious services, including Mass and the Liturgy of the Hours. The monks operate a guesthouse which is open to those individuals who wish to experience a time of prayer and silence.

Neuzelle Kloster

Stiftsplatz 5
15898 Neuzelle (Frankfurt-an-der-Oder)
Tel/Fax: (033652) 282

Founded in 1268, the Cloister of Neuzelle is home to a community of Premonstratensian Canons (Norbertine Fathers). Inside the artistically rich abbey church, visitors can join the monks in their daily life of prayer, including Mass. A diocesan guesthouse is located near the abbey, providing accommodation to both men and women who are visiting the monastery. There are concerts featuring both classical and sacred music throughout the year at the abbey.

Benediktinerabtei

Sebastian-Kneipp-Str. 1
87724 Ottobeuren
Tel: (08332) 79-80 • Fax: (08332) 798-120

Founded in the eighth century, Ottobeuren Abbey is home to a community of Benedictine monks. Welcoming visitors and tourists from all over the world, the abbey features a vast basilica that is virtually unmatched for its interior beauty and majestic spaciousness. As well as exploring the immense church, the faithful can spend time in the well-appointed museum, attend religious services, and visit the abbey gift shop. Guided tours of the abbey are available, but you should make reservations in advance. Although guest rooms are not available, there is  a tourist office located across the street which can help arrange accommodation close to the monastery. For more information, contact them at:

Kurverwaltung-Haus des Gastes
Marktplatz 14
87724 Ottobeuren
Tel: (08332) 92-19-52, 92-19-53, 92-19-50
Fax: (08332) 92-19-92
E-mail: touristikamt@ottobeuren.de
Web Site: www.ottobeuren.de

Benediktinerabtei zum Heiligen Kreuz
Schyrenplatz 1
85297 Scheyern (Pfaffenhofen)
Tel (Abbey): (08441) 752-0
Tel (Guesthouse): (08441) 752-230
Fax: (08441) 752-210

Founded in 1119, the Abbey of Heiligen Kreuz is home to a community of Benedictine monks. Visitors are welcome to join the monks at religious services in the abbey church, as well as participate in the summertime processions to honoring the Holy Cross. The monastery operates an excellent guesthouse called *Schyren-Hof*, which provides accommodation for both men and women. Concerts featuring both classical and sacred music take place throughout the year at the abbey.

Abtei Saint Matthias
Matthiasstrasse 85
54290 Trier
Tel: (0651) 31-079 • Fax: (0651) 359-69

Founded in 1148, the Abbey of Saint Matthias is home to a community of Benedictine monks. Located on the outskirts of Trier, the monastery receives thousands of pilgrims annually for one main reason—the sacred relics of the apostle Saint Matthias are enshrined here. As well as attending religious services with the monks, the faithful can

visit the abbey museum which houses an extensive collection of artifacts, paintings, and historical documents. The feast day of Saint Matthias is celebrated annually on May 14, with many pilgrims arriving for the great day of festivities. Although the abbey does not provide a guesthouse for visitors, there is a convent nearby (located in the center of Trier; a short bus ride from the abbey) which does accommodate individuals seeking a time of prayer and retreat. For more information, or to make reservations, you may contact them: Sisters of Saint Joseph Convent, Josefsstift Trier, Franz-LudwigStrasse 7, 54290 Trier, Tel: (0651) 9769-0, Fax: (0651) 9769-111.

GREECE

SERVING AS THE center of Eastern Orthodox Monasticism, Mount Athos has long been considered one of the most famous monastic sites in Europe. With only monks registered as its permanent residents, today the city is the only place in Greece to be completely dedicated to prayer and the worship of God. Covering an area of approximately two hundred square miles, Mount Athos lies on the beautiful Halkidiki peninsula in the northeastern section of the country, and is comprised of about twenty monasteries.

According to Orthodox Christian tradition, the founding of Mount Athos dates back to the first century. It is said that Saint John the Evangelist and the Blessed Virgin Mary discovered the area when they were forced to take refuge there during a storm on their travels to Cyprus to visit Lazarus. Struck by the beauty of the land, the Blessed Virgin asked God to offer the mountain to them as a gift. After presenting the petition to the Lord, she then heard God reply: "Let this place be your lot, your garden and your paradise, as well as a salvation, a haven for those who seek salvation." Ever since that time, Mount Athos has been referred to as *The Garden of the Virgin Mary*. However, it wasn't until the fifth century that the first monks arrived at Mount Athos to establish their monasteries.

Today, Mount Athos serves as a self-governed city in Greece, but it is subject to the Ministry of Foreign Affairs in political matters, and subject to the Ecumenical Patriarch of Constantinople in religious matters. The entire municipality is divided into twenty self-governed territories, each one consisting of a cardinal monastery with other monastic establishments surrounding it (cloisters, cells, cottages, hermitages, and so on).

Each monastery is governed by a superior who presides over the affairs of the community and is elected for life. The superiors are also members of the Holy Assembly which exercises its legislative authority over all of Mount Athos. Within each monastery, the activities of the monks are performed in community, including the liturgy, prayer, manual labor, housing, and eating.

In compliance with a long-standing tradition, only men are allowed to visit Mount Athos (and its monasteries). In order to visit the city, you must first apply for a permit and then make reservations with one of the following:

1. Pilgrim's Office of Athos, 9 Egnatia Saint, Thessaloniki (Tel: 031/ 861-611; Fax: 031/861-811)
2. American Consulate in Thessalonika (Tel: 031/242-905; Fax: 031/ 242-927)
3. American Embassy in Athens (Tel: 01/721-2951, Fax: 01/645-6282)
4. Or contact the Greek National Tourist Organization within your country to obtain the latest phone and fax numbers (or e-mail address) of those offices providing the permits

These bookings/inquiries must be made at least two weeks prior to your visit, since the number of visitors to Mount Athos is limited. Once your reservation is confirmed, you will receive a code number which will serve as your permit. The number of permits issued daily is limited to about one hundred and twenty.

The Pilgrim's Office charges a fee for the permit, which usually allows for a three-night stay, and includes both lodging and food at the monasteries. Overnight stays are allowed only for those individuals with a proven religious or scientific interest in the area and who are over eighteen years of age.

To obtain more detailed information about Mount Athos, be sure to visit the following Web sites:

• http://www.inathos.gr
• http://www.medialab.ntua.gr/athos.html

The following is a brief outline of each of the twenty Mount Athos monasteries. Please note the phrase "second account" included with some entries which indicates that an alternate source provided additional/ contradictory information:

1. Holy Monastery of Zografos
   Foundation: tenth century
   Founders: monk Moses, monk Aaron and monk Ioannis
   Dedication: to Saint George
   Celebration: April 23
   Accommodation: large guesthouse

2. Holy Monastery of Kastamonitis
   Foundation: fourth century
   Founder: Constantine the Great
   Dedication: to Saint Stephen
   Celebration: December 27
      Second account:
      Foundation: eleventh century
      Founder: monk Kastamonitis
      Accommodation: large guesthouse

3. Holy Monastery of Dochiarios
   Foundation: tenth century
   Founder: monk Efthimios
   Dedication: to the Archangels Michael and Gabriel
   Celebration: November 8
   Accommodation: modest guesthouse

4. Holy Monastery of Xenophon
   Foundation: tenth century
   Founder: Saint Xenophon
   Dedication: to Saint George
   Celebration: April 23
   Accommodation: large guesthouse

5. Holy Monastery of Panteleimon
   Foundation: eleventh century
   Founders: Russian monks
   Dedication: to Saint Panteleimon
   Celebration: July 27
   Accommodation: guesthouse; Russian pilgrims especially welcomed

6. Holy Monastery of Xiropotamos
   Foundation: fifth century
   Founder: Empress Pulcheria
   Dedication: to the 40 martyrs
   Celebration: March 9
      Second account:
      Foundation: tenth century
      Founders: monk Pavlos Xeropotaminos
      Accommodation: large guesthouse

7. Holy Monastery of Simon Petras
   Foundation: thirteenth century
   Founder: Saint Simon
   Dedication: to the birth of Jesus
   Celebration: December 25
   Accommodation: guesthouse has spectacular panoramic views

8. Holy Monastery of Gregorios
   Foundation: fourteenth century
   Founder: Gregory of Sinai
   Dedication: to Saint Nikolaos
   Celebration: December 6
   > Second account:
   > Founder: Gregorios from Syriana
   > Accommodation: large guesthouse

9. Holy Monastery of Dionysos
   Foundation: fourteenth century
   Founders: Saint Dionysios
   Dedication: to the birth of the honorable Saint John the Baptist
   Celebration: June 24
   Accommodation: very comfortable guesthouse with meals served in the monks splendid refectory

10. Holy Monastery of Saint (Agios) Pavlos
    Foundation: eighth century
    Founder: Saint Pavlos
    Dedication: to the Candlemas of Jesus
    Celebration: February 2
    > Second account:
    > Foundation: tenth century
    > Founder: Pavlos Xeropotaminos
    > Accommodation: comfortable guesthouse

11. Holy Monastery of Megisti Lavra
    Foundation: A.D. 963
    Founder: monk Athanasios
    Dedication: Dormition of Athanasios
    Celebration: July 5
    Accommodation: welcoming guesthouse

12. Holy Monastery of Karakalos
    Foundation: third century
    Founder: Empress Karakalla
    Dedication: to Peter and Paul, Apostles
    Celebration: June 29
       Second account:
       Foundation: eleventh century
       Founder: monk Karakalas
       Accommodation: large guesthouse

13. Holy Monastery of Filotheos
    Foundation: tenth century
    Founder: Saint Filotheos
    Dedication: to the Annunciation of the Mother of God
    Celebration: March 25
    Accommodation: large guesthouse

14. Holy Monastery of Iviron
    Foundation: tenth century
    Founders: Ioannis the Ivir and Ioannis the Tornikios
    Dedication: Assumption of the Mother of God
    Celebration: August 15

15. Holy Monastery of Koutloumousion
    Foundation: tenth century
    Founder: Koutloumous
    Dedication: to the Transfiguration of Christ
    Celebration: August 6
    Accommodation: large guesthouse

16. Holy Monastery of Stayronikitas
    Foundation: tenth century
    Founder: Nikiforos Stavronikitas
    Dedication: to Saint Nikolaos
    Celebration: December 6
       Second account:
       Founder: patrician Nikitas
       Accommodation: large guesthouse

17. Holy Monastery of Pantokrator
    Foundation: fourteenth century
    Founders: monk Alexios and monk Ioannis
    Dedication: to the Transfiguration of Christ
    Celebration: August 6
    Accommodation: large guesthouse

18. Holy Monastery of Vatopedion
    Foundation: fourth century
    Founder: Emperor Theodosios A'
    Dedication: to the Annunciation of the Mother of God
    Celebration: March 25
        Second account:
        Foundation: between 972 and 985
        Founders: monk Athanasios, monk Nikolaos, monk Antonios
    Accommodation: large guesthouse

19. Holy Monastery of Esfigmrnos
    Foundation: fifth century
    Founders: Emperor Theodosios B'
    Dedication: to the Ascension of Jesus Christ
    Celebration: Forty days after Easter
        Second account:
        Foundation: tenth century
    Accommodation: large guesthouse

20. Holy Monastery of Helandarion
    Foundation: tenth century
    Founder: Helandarios
    Dedication: to the Presentation of the Virgin Mary
    Celebration: November 21
    Accommodation: large guesthouse

Note: Information about the above monasteries provided by the Mount Athos Web site.

HUNGARY

Jézus Szive Noverék Társasága

Wlassics Gyula u. 84/b
1181 Budapest
Tel/Fax: (01) 290-9674

Founded in 1993, this Hungarian abbey is home to the newly established Society of Adoration of the Sacred Heart monks. As well as spending time in the church, the faithful can join the monks in Mass and Eucharistic Adoration. Students, families, groups, and consecrated religious are all welcome to stay for a few days in the guesthouse (if available).

Ciszterci Novérek Boldogassznoy Háza Monostor

2623 Kismaros (Vác)
Tel: (027) 350-306, 350-307 • Fax: (027) 350-029

Founded in 1955, the abbey is home to a community of Cistercian monks. Annually, the monastery receives several thousand students and pilgrims who come to attend religious services with the monks, and to pray in the newly built monastery church (1993). Guests traveling independently or in groups can be accommodated in the abbey guesthouse, but they must come with the desire to participate more fully in the prayer life of the monastery.

IRELAND

$$\begin{array}{c} + \| + \\ \hline + \| + \end{array}$$

Saint Benedict's Priory
The Mount
Cobh
Co. Cork

Founded in 1916, Saint Benedict's Priory offers the visitor an incredible array of monastic hospitality. As well as spending time in retreat, guests can visit the Irish Monastic Heritage Center, the Bible Garden, and the shrine of Saint Oliver Plunkett. The Bible Garden, contains more than an acre of species of trees, shrubs, plants, and flowers that are named in the Bible. Time can also be spent praying the monastic liturgy of the Hours with the Benedictine Oblate sisters, as well as attending Mass and Eucharistic Adoration. The monastic guesthouse has six single rooms, and two double rooms.

Convent of Saint Mary Immaculate of the Rosary
Tallaght—Dublin 24
Dublin

Founded in 1865, the Convent of Saint Mary Immaculate is home to a community of Dominican nuns. Visitors can attend Mass in the convent chapel (built in 1886), and join in one of many prayer groups. The feast days of Saint Thomas Aquinas (January 28), Saint Dominic (August 8), and Our Lady of the Rosary (October 7) are celebrated at the chapel. The nuns operate an excellent guesthouse called *The Dominican Retreat and Pastoral Center*, which has forty bedrooms (thirty-five singles, five doubles), a conference room, restaurant, and garden. Men, women, and young people are welcome to stay at the guesthouse, which include facilities for the handicapped. Concerts of both classical and sacred music take place throughout the year at the convent.

Bolton Abbey

Moone (Athy)
Co. Kildare
Tel: (0507) 241-02 • Tel/Fax: (0507) 24-309
E-mail: boltonabbey@eircom.net

Founded in 1965, Bolton Abbey is home to a community of thirteen Cistercian monks, whose primary means of livelihood is dairy farming. As well as spending time in retreat and attending the monks' Liturgy of the Hours, guests can visit the remains of the Celtic monasteries of Moone and Castledermot—famous for their high crosses—which is close by. Accommodation in one of the eight monastic guest rooms should be confirmed with the guestmaster at least one month before the expected date of arrival. The most convenient times for phoning/faxing the monastery are between 10:30–11:30 A.M. and 6:00–7:00 P.M. Irish time).

Glenstal Abbey

Murroe
Co. Limerick
Tel: (061) 386-103 • Fax: (061) 386-328
E-mail: glenstal@iol.ie
Web Site: www.glenstal.ie

Originally founded in 1927, the Benedictine abbey of Glenstal has continued to grow over the years and today houses almost fifty monks. Among their numerous apostolic works, the monks run a large farming enterprise which is primarily devoted to milk production. Also involved in academics and lecturing, they operate a guesthouse that can accommodate more than three thousand visitors each year.

Kylemore Abbey

Kylemore (Connemara)
Co. Galway
Tel: (095) 411-46 • Fax: (095) 411-23
Tel/Fax: (01) 289-94-87
E-mail: bbrew@kylemoreabbey.ie
oflaherty@cyberclub.iol.ie
Web Site: www.kylemoreabbey.com

Welcoming visitors from around the world, Kylemore Abbey is home to a community of Irish Benedictine nuns whose founding dates back to 1665. A popular destination for both tourists and religious pilgrims, the abbey features a visitors' center, craft and pottery shop, restaurant, and beautiful gardens. Guest rooms are available for those visitors who wish to experience the monastic life.

Mount Saint Joseph Abbey

Roscrea (Limerick)
Co. Tipperary
Tel: (0505) 21-711 • Fax: (0505) 22-198
E-mail: mtjoseph@iol.ie
Web Site: http://ireland.iol.ie/~mtjoseph

Located in the midst of many ancient Celtic monastic sites and medieval ruins, Mount Saint Joseph Abbey was founded in 1878 by thirty Cistercian monks. Today, the monks operate a farm, boarding school, and a guesthouse which accommodates about forty people. Fresh home-baked bread is just one of the many ways the monks extend a hearty welcome to all who come to spend a few days in retreat and participate in their daily lives.

ITALY

Abbazia di Monte Oliveto Maggiore

Località Chiusure—Monte Oliveto
53020 Asciano (Siena)
Tel: (0577) 707-017 • Fax: (0577) 707-070
E-mail: momdon@ftbcc.it
Web Site: www.ftbcc.it/monteoliveto

Recognized as one of the early foundations of the Benedictine Olivetan Order, the abbey of Monte Oliveto Maggiore dates back to 1313. For centuries, the monastery has held a foremost position in the fields of science and art. Recently, they opened a school for the restoration of old books. Guest rooms are available to those individuals or groups who wish to participate in a spiritual retreat or personal days of reflection. The guesthouse is closed during the winter.

Abbazia Sacra di San Michele

Padri Rosminiani
10051 Avigliana
Tel/Fax: (011) 939-130
E-mail: info@sacradisanmichele.com
Web Site: www.sacradisanmichele.com

An architectural and natural wonder, the abbey and shrine of Saint Michael today serves as one of the most famous Benedictine monasteries from Medieval Europe, dating back almost one thousand years. Sitting atop the rocky, chiseled summit of Mount Pirchiriano, the monastery has a number of sites to interest the religious visitor including the Monk's Tomb, the Stairway of the Dead, and the Primitive Shrine of Saint Michael. Since the abbey can only accommodate two or three visitors at a time (men or women), guests must stay for a period of at least three to five days, and be willing to participate in the prayer life of the monastery. Only Italian is spoken at the abbey. The guesthouse is open throughout the year, except between the periods: July 1 to September 15; and December 15 to January 15.

Monastero San Vincenzo Martire

Monaci Benedettini Silvestrini
Via San Vincenzo, 88
01030 Bassano Romano (VT)
Tel: (0761) 634-007, (0761) 634-086 • Fax: (0761) 634-734
E-mail: sanvincenzo@silvestrini.org
Web Site: http://sanvincenzo.silvestrini.org

Built in 1630, the monastery of Benedettini Silvestrini is home to a community of Benedictine monks. As well as spending time in the abbey, visitors can pray at the shrine of Santo Volto, a center for spirituality, which is located next to the monastery. The monks operate a vast guesthouse which provides accommodation for more than three hundred people.

Abbazia di San Petro di Sorres

Località San Pietro di Sorres
07040 Borutta (Sassari)
Tel: (079) 824-001 • Fax: (079) 824-019
Web Site: http://diocesioristano.freeservers.com/sorres.htm

Founded in the eleventh century, the Abbey of San Petro di Sorres is home to a community of monks who belong to the Benedictine Congregation of Subiaco. The faithful can participate in the liturgical life of the monks, including Mass and the Liturgy of the Hours. Major feast days celebrated at the monastery include Saint Peter (June 29), Saint Benedict (July 11), and the Birth of the Virgin Mary (September 8). Guest rooms are available to those individuals who wish to participate in a personal retreat of prayer and silence.

Abbazia Santa Maria Assunta di Praglia

35033 Bresseo di Teolo (Padova)
Tel: (049) 99-00-010 • Fax: (049) 99-02-740
E-mail: abbazia@tin.it

Founded in the twelfth century, Saint Mary's Abbey is home to a community of forty Benedictine monks. As well as visiting the vast monastery, the faithful can spend time in retreat by attending the monks' Liturgy of the Hours (sung in Gregorian chant). Men wishing to participate in the life of the monks can stay in one of the guest rooms which are located on the interior of the monastery, while women and groups can stay in one of the ten small "apartments" on the exterior. At the abbey gift shop, visitors may purchase such items as honey, herbs, ointments, soaps, cosmetic creams, and liqueurs, most of which are produced by the monks themselves.

Abbazia di Montecassino

03043 Cassino (Frosinone)
Tel: (0776) 311-529 • Fax: (0776) 312-393
Web Site: www.officine.it/montecassino

Founded by Saint Benedict about the year 529, the Abbey of Montecassino has, through the centuries, garnered a worldwide reputation for being a place of holiness, culture, and art. Many great historic figures have visited the monastery, including Charlemagne who, in 787, bestowed many privileges and gifts upon the abbey. Reduced to rubble during World War II, the abbey was quickly rebuilt in accordance with the ancient architectural pattern. Only men can be accommodated in the guest rooms; advance reservations are required.

Abbazia di Santa Fede

Via Santa Fede 92
10020 Cavagnolo (Torino)
Tel: (011) 915-11-24

Founded in the twelfth century, the Abbey of Santa Fede is home to a community of Marist Fathers. Visitors can be accommodated in one of the guest rooms, and are invited to participate in the spiritual retreats of the house.

Convento Cappuccini

Santuario Maria SS. di Gibilmanna
90010 Gibilmanna-Cefalù (Palermo)
Tel: (0921) 421-835 • Fax: (0921) 422-221
E-mail: gibilmanna.sanctuario@tiscalinet.it

Founded in 1535, the Convent and Sanctuary of Maria Santissima di Gibilmanna is home to a community of Capuchin Friars Minor. As well as praying before a miraculous image of the Virgin Mary located inside the shrine, visitors can join the monks in their daily life of prayer in the abbey church. The Saint Clare guesthouse is open to all individuals, families, and groups who wish to embark on a spiritual retreat or a time of prayer and solitude. Many musical concerts, Marian processions, and religious celebrations take place throughout the year at both the sanctuary and abbey.

Convento-santuari de la Verna

Località La Verna
52010 Chiusi della Verna (Arezzo)
Tel: (0575) 5341 • Fax: (0575) 599-320

Founded in 1213, the Convent and Sanctuary of Verna is home to a community of Franciscan Minors. Among the most famous site to visit at the monastery and shrine is the renowned Chapel of the Stigmata. Religious celebrations and eucharistic processions are held throughout the year. The Franciscans operate a very large guesthouse, which is open to both men and women (120 beds are available). Organ concerts take place in July and August at the shrine.

Monastero di San Silvestro

Via San Silvestro Abate 66
60044 Fabriano (Ancona)

Founded in 1231, the Monastery of San Silvestro is home to a community of Benedictine monks. As well as touring the abbey, visitors can attend Mass in the monastery church. A modern, well-equipped guesthouse provides accommodation (thirty-five rooms) to those individuals who wish to participate in a personal retreat of prayer and recollection.

Eremo di Monte Giove

Via Rosciano 90
61032 Fano (Pesaro-Urbino)
Tel (Hermitage): (0721) 864-090 • Tel (Guesthouse): (0721) 864-603
Fax: (0721) 864-603

Built in the seventeenth century, the hermitage of Monte Giove is home to a community of Benedictine monks. Visitors are welcome to join the monks at Mass, the Liturgy of the Hours, spiritual retreats, and in days of prayer. Among the most popular feast days at the abbey are those celebrations that honor Saint Benedict (March 21 and July 11), Saint Romuald (June 19), and the Feast of the Transfiguration (August 6). A guesthouse with forty rooms is available only to those individuals and groups who want to participate in the prayer life of the hermitage.

Abbazia di Santa Maria

Via Santuario 59—Finale Pia
17024 Finale Ligure
Tel: (019) 601-700 • Fax: (019) 601-912

Founded in 1477, the Abbey of Santa Maria is home to a community of monks which belong to the Benedictine Congregation of Subiaco. Visitors can tour the beautiful abbey church which has a number of frescoes and sculptures, as well as other religious artwork. The faithful are invited to join the monks at Mass and to participate in the abbey's conferences and spiritual retreats. The monastery guesthouse, *Villa Enrichetta*, provides accommodation to those individuals and families who are seeking a time of prayer and silence.

Convento di Sant'Anna

Piazza Sant'Anna 8
16125 Genova
Tel: (010) 277-0433 • Fax: (010) 251-3281
E-mail: carmelo@split.it

Founded in 1584, the Convent of Sant'Anna is home to a community of Carmelite monks. Visitors are invited to attend religious services, which include Mass and the Liturgy of the Hours. Among the most important feast days celebrated at the abbey are those honoring Our Lady of Mount Carmel (July 16), Saint Anne (July 26), Saint Thérèse of Lisieux (October 1), Saint Térèse of Avila (October 15), and Saint John of the Cross (December 14). Individuals and small groups can be accommodated in the Carmelite guesthouse which has ten rooms. Organ concerts are given throughout the year, especially during the community's major feast days.

Abbazia S. Maria della Castagna

Via Romana della Castagna, 11
16148 Genova-Quarto
Tel: (010) 399-0996 • Fax: (010) 377-8227
E-mail: abbazia.castagna@libero.it

Founded in 1843, the Abbey of Santa Maria della Castagna is home to a community of Benedictine monks. As well as touring the abbey church and grounds, visitors are invited to participate in the prayer life of the monks. A guesthouse provides accommodation for twenty-one people (seven singles, seven doubles).

Convento–Santuario della Madonna di Barbana
Isola de Barbana
34073 Grado (Gorizia)
Tel: (0431) 804-53

Founded in 582, the Convent of Madonna di Barbana is home to a community of Franciscan Minors. Welcoming thousands of pilgrims annually, the Franciscans serve as custodians of this Marian shrine, which houses a miraculous image of the Blessed Virgin Mary. The Franciscans also operate the Pilgrim's Guesthouse, which provides accommodation for both individuals and groups (twenty-four rooms are available). Many religious processions and celebrations are held throughout the year at the shrine.

Abbazia di Chiaravalle
Via San Arialdo 102
20139 Milano
Tel: (02) 574-03-404

Founded by Saint Bernard of Clairvaux in 1135, the Abbey of Chiaravalle is home to a community of twenty-two Cistercian monks. As well as touring the beautiful abbey church with its many frescoes and works of art, visitors can attend religious services with the monks. Annually, on August 20, there is a solemn High Pontifical Mass to honor Saint Bernard. Since the twelve guest rooms are located inside the monastic enclosure, only men can be housed for an overnight stay.

Abbazia Madonna della Scala

Contrada Z.B. 58
70015 Noci (Bari)
Tel: (080) 847-5838, (080) 847-5839

Founded in 1930, the Abbey of Madonna della Scala is home to a community of monks that belong to the Benedictine Congregation of Subiaco. Religious services, including Mass and the Liturgy of the Hours, take place in the abbey church and are open to the public. Only men can be accommodated in the abbey guest rooms, since they are located inside the monastic enclosure. Courses to learn Gregorian chant are offered during the summer.

Abbazia di San Giovanni Evangelista

Piazzale San Giovanni Evangelista 1
43100 Parma
Tel: (0521) 235-592

Founded in 1144, the Abbey of San Giovanni Evangelista is home to a community of Benedictine monks. As well as touring the impressive abbey church, the faithful are invited to participate in the prayer life of the monks. Only those men who seek a time of personal retreat in a monastic environment can be accommodated.

Monastero di Camaldoli

Località Camaldoli
52010 Poppi (Arezzo)
Tel: (0575) 556-012 • Fax: (0575) 556-001
Web Site: www.camaldoli.it

Founded almost a thousand years ago, the Abbey of Camaldoli is home to a community of Camaldolese Benedictine monks. Visitors are invited to attend religious services with the monks, and to participate in the many retreats and seminars that are held each year at the monastery which are based upon the theme of ecumenism and interreligious dialogue. A well-appointed guesthouse is available to both men and women who wish to participate in either a traditional silent retreat, or a course offered by the monks.

Abbazia di Vallombrosa

Località Vallombrosa
50060 Reggello (Firenze)
Tel (Abbey): (055) 862-029
Tel (Guesthouse): (055) 862-074 (only available during the summer)

Founded in 1028, the Abbey of Vallmobrosa is home to a community of Benedictine monks. Guided tours of the abbey are available to groups during the summer. All visitors are welcome to attend religious services with the monks in the church. The monks operate a very large guesthouse for those individuals and groups who wish to embark on a monastic retreat of prayer and solitude. Organ concerts are held during the months of July and August.

Convento–Santuario di Santa Maria dei Lattani

Località Monte Lattani
81035 Roccamonfina (Caserta)
Tel: (0823) 921-037

Founded in 1430, the Convent of Santa Maria dei Lattani is home to a community of Franciscan Minors. Many pilgrims come here annually to pray in the abbey shrine, which has a miraculous image of the Blessed Virgin Mary. Men can be accommodated in the monastery guesthouse, while women and families can be accommodated in the nearby sanctuary hotel. All are invited to participate in religious services at the abbey and sanctuary.

Abbazia di San Michele

Sacra di San Michele
10057 Sant'Ambrogio Torinese (Torino)
Tel: (011) 939-130

Founded almost a thousand years ago, the Abbey of San Michele is home to a community of Rosminiani Fathers. Visitors and guests are welcome to attend Mass, as well as the spiritual conferences held at the monastery throughout the year. Faithful to its vocation, the abbey offers excellent accommodations for those individuals who wish to participate in a spiritual retreat. Reservations are recommended, since there are only four or five rooms available.

Abbazia dei Santi Pietro e Paolo in Viboldone

Via della Abbazia 6
20098 San Giuliano Milanese (Milano)
Tel: (02) 984-1203 • Fax: (02) 982-2409-43

Originally founded in 1176, today the abbey of Santi Pietro e Paolo is home to a community of Benedictine monks who revived the monastery in 1941. The faithful are welcome to join the monks in their daily life of prayer in the abbey church, which includes Mass and the Liturgy of the Hours. Ten guest rooms are available to individuals and small groups who wish to spend time in prayer and reflection in a monastic environment. Many organ, Gregorian chant, and polyphonic music concerts are held at the abbey throughout the year.

Abbazia di San Martino delle Scale

Piazza Platani 5
90040 San Martino delle Scale (Palermo)
Tel: (091) 418-104

Founded in 590, the Abbey of San Martino delle Scale is home to a community of monks who belong to the Benedictine Congregation of Monte Cassino. As well as exploring the ancient abbey church, all visitors are invited to participate in religious services, which include Mass and the Divine Office (sung in Gregorian chant). Individuals and small groups seeking a spiritual retreat are welcome to spend several days at the abbey (ten guest rooms are available inside the monastic enclosure and five guest rooms on the exterior). During July and August, symphonic concerts are held within the abbey cloister, and organ concerts are held in the church.

Abbazia S. Benedetto

Via Stefano da Seregno, 100
20038 Seregno (Milano)
Tel: (0362) 23-17-72, (0362) 23-95-11
Fax: (0362) 23-17-72, (0362) 32-11-30

Founded in the fourteenth century, today Saint Benedict's Abbey is home to a community of Benedictine monks. All visitors are invited to participate in the prayer life of the monks, which includes both Mass and the Liturgy of the Hours. Guest rooms, located on the exterior of the monastery, are available, while guest rooms inside the monastery are occasionally available to young people who wish to experience the monastic life firsthand. If this is the case, as a requirement for admission, a letter from a priest explaining your intention must be sent prior to your visit to the Father Abbot. Honey, jelly, liquors, and medicines are all available at the porter's lodge.

Monastero S. Scolastica

Casa per Esercizi Spirituali
Località Santa Scholastica
00028 Subiaco (Roma)
Tel: (0744) 855-69 • Fax: (0744) 822-862
Web Site: www.benedettini-subiaco.it

Serving as one of the thirteen monasteries founded by Saint Benedict (480–547) in the area of Subiaco, the abbey of Saint Scholastica is one of Europe's most famous monastic pilgrimage sites. The monastery's guesthouse offers very comfortable accommodations and excellent hospitality to independent or group travelers who wish to participate in the spiritual exercises and life of the monks.

Monastero di Santa Maria della Neve

43010 Torrechiara (Parme)
Tel: (052) 355-178

Founded in 1471, the Monastery of Santa Maria della Neve is home to a community of monks who belong to the Benedictine Congregation of Subiaco. Visitors are welcome to participate in religious services, which include Mass and the Liturgy of the Hours. The major annual religious celebrations at the abbey are March 21 and July 11, the feast days of Saint Benedict. The monastery guesthouse has more than twenty-four rooms for adults, as well as a dormitory for groups of young people.

Bildungshaus Kloster Neustift

Stiftstr. 1
39040 Vahrn/Varna
Tel: (0472) 835-588 • Fax: (0472) 838-107
E-mail: bildungshaus@kloster-neustift.it
Web Site: www.kloster-neustift.it

Founded in 1142 as the region's spiritual and religious center, this Augustinian monastery has, for centuries, attracted large numbers of pilgrims who seek lodging while on their journeys to either the Holy Land or Rome. On a tour, guests can visit the abbey's famous cloister, library, church, museum, and wine cellar. Although there is no gift shop, you can purchase the abbey's wines and herb teas. The monastery's convention and education center provides housing (forty-nine beds) to those groups who either give their own seminars or to individuals who join the in-house courses and events. The mailing address and phone/fax numbers for the convention and education center are:

Bildungshaus Kloster Neustift
Stiftstraße 1 - Via Abbazia 1I-39042
Brixen - Bressanone
Tel: (0472) 83-61-89, 83-55-88
Fax: (0472) 83-73-05, 83-81-07

Abbazia di Casamari

Frazione di Casamari
03020 Veroli (Frosinone)
Tel: (0775) 282-800

Built in 1035, today the Abbey of Casamari is home to a community of Cistercian monks. As well as taking tours of the ancient and beautiful church, visitors can attend religious services with the monks. Although only men can be accommodated inside the monastic enclosure, women can be accommodated in a nearby guesthouse (reservations are required for both). Music concerts and exhibitions are held throughout the year at the monastery.

Abbaye Saint-Maurice

9737 Clervaux
Grand-Duché de Luxembourg
Tel: (0352) 921-027 • Fax: (0352) 920-144

Refounded in 1890, the Abbey of Saint Maurice is home to a community of Benedictine monks who are a part of the Congregation of Solesmes. All are invited to participate in the monks' daily life of prayer, especially Mass and Liturgy of the Hours, which are sung in Gregorian chant. Twenty guest rooms are available for men inside the abbey, and housing can possibly be provided for youth groups and women. Visitors can purchase such items as books, religious art, Gregorian chant CDs, and cassettes at the abbey gift shop.

Carmel

10, rue Sainte-Thérèse-d'Avila
1152 Luxembourg
Tel: (0352) 43-16-31 • Fax: (0352) 42-18-28

Founded in 1889, this Luxembourg convent is home to a community of Carmelite nuns. Four guest rooms are available to those individuals who want to participate in a personal retreat of prayer and silence. Visitors are welcome to attend Mass and the Divine Office in the convent chapel, which is said in French.

Monastère des Bénédictines du Saint-Sacrement

3, rue Saint-Benoît
3391 Peppange
Tel: (0352) 51-10-61 • Fax: (0352) 51-06-08

Founded in 1875, the Monastery of Saint-Sacrement is home to a community of Benedictine monks. The abbey's Mass and Liturgy of the Hours are open to the public, all visitors are welcome to attend. A limited number of guest rooms are available to those individuals who wish to participate in a personal retreat of prayer and silence.

$$\frac{+\|+}{+\|+}$$

Abdij O.L. Vrouw van Koningshoeven

Notre-Dame de Koningshoeven
Eindhovenseweg 3
5056 RP Berkel-Enschot
Tel: (013) 543-61-24 • Fax: (013) 544-36-78
Web Site: www.koningshoeven.nl

Founded in the nineteenth century, the Abbey of Koningshoeven is home to a community of eleven Trappist monks. Since the monastery is situated on land that was not originally suitable for farming, from early on, the monks resorted to brewing beer for their livelihood. Today, their brewery remains the single most important source of revenue for the abbey. Guest rooms are available to men and women who wish to participate in the prayer life of the monks, and spend a few days in personal retreat.

Sint Willibrordsabdij

Slangenburg, Abdijlaan 1
7004 JL Doetinchem
Tel: (0315) 29-82-68
Web Site: www.willibrords-abbey.nl

Founded in 1945, the Benedictine Abbey of Saint Willibrords lies in a beautiful setting of forest and woods. As well as leading a contemplative life of prayer, study, and hospitality, the monks devote themselves to the manufacture of liturgical vestments, and the preservation of valuable and rare old religious books. Visitors can spend several days in retreat at the abbey guesthouse, *Castle Slangenburg.*

Sint Adalbertabdij

Benedictijner Monniken
Abdijlaan 26
1935 BH Egmond-Binnen
Tel: (072) 506-14-15 • Fax: (072) 506-48-34
E-mail: klooster@abdijkaarsen.nl
Web Site: www.abdijkaarsen.nl

Founded in 950, the Abbey of Saint Adalbert is home to a community of Benedictine monks. As well as visiting the large and austere monastery church, visitors can participate in religious services with the monks, including Mass. The most popular feast days at the abbey include celebrations honoring Saint Benedict (March 21 and July 11), Saint Adalbert (June 20), and the Consecration of the Monastery (October 7). The monastery operates a guesthouse with twelve rooms. It is available to those individuals who wish to participate more fully in the prayer life of the monks. One of the major activities of the monks is the production of candles.

Klooster Sint Josephsberg

Clarastraat 2
5366 AK Megen
Fax: (0412) 46-31-20

Founded in 1721, the Convent of Saint Josephberg is home to a community of Poor Clare nuns. Mass is celebrated daily, and the most popular feast day at the chapel is August 11 (Saint Clare of Assisi). The nuns operate a small guesthouse with eight rooms for both men and women who seek a place of prayer and silence.

Priorij Fons Vitae

Benedictuslaan 7
5343 NB Oss
Fax: (0412) 45-36-01

Founded in 1952, the Priory of Fons Vitae is home to a community of Benedictine monks of the Holy Sacrament. A guesthouse is available to those individuals who wish to participate in a personal retreat in a monastic environment. Only five or six people can be accommodated at one time, and everyone is expected to join the monks in their prayer life, which includes Mass and the Divine Office. Candles, ceramics, and religious icons are just a few of the items that you may purchase at the priory.

Sint–Paulus Abdij

Hoogstraat 80
4901 PK Oosterhout
Tel: (0162) 45-33-94 • Fax: (0162) 42-53-11

Founded in 1907, the Abbey of Sint-Paulus is home to a community of Benedictine monks. Visitors are welcome to attend Mass in the chapel, as well as the Liturgy of the Hours. Since the guesthouse is very small, only men who want to spend a few days in prayer and silence can be accommodated. The monks produce artistic ceramics.

Saint Benedictus Abdij De Achelse Kluis

Abdijweg 50
5556 VE Valkenswaard
Tel (Abbey): (011) 800-760 • Tel (Guesthouse): (011) 800-766
Fax: (011) 648-130
Web Site: www.achelsekluis.nl

Founded in 1686, the Abbey of Achelse Kluis is home to a community of Cistercian monks. Serving as a place of prayer and contemplation, the monastery invites all visitors to join them in the chapel for Mass and the singing of the Divine Office. The monastery guesthouse receives both men and women, providing an opportunity for individuals to join the monks in their prayerful rhythm of life.

Lunden Kloster

Monastery of the Annunciation
Ovre Lunden 5
0594 Oslo
Tel: (047) 22-64-18-20 • Fax: (047) 22-65-57-90
Web Site: www.katolsk.no/ordener/lunden_e.htm
http://lunden.katolsk.no

Founded in 1951, the Monastery of the Annunciation is comprised of eleven nuns who belong to the contemplative branch of the Dominican Order. The monastery has a guesthouse with six rooms. Visitors are encouraged to participate in the daily Office, which is sung in both Norwegian and Gregorian chant. You may purchase candles, icons, rosaries, cards, books, and other religious articles from the sisters.

Utstein Kloster

4000 Utstein (Stavanger)
Tel: (04) 51-72-47-05 • Fax: (04) 51-72-47-08

Originally founded in 1270, then restored in 1965, the Abbey of Utstein is home to a community of Augustinian monks. As well as attending religious services with the monks, visitors can spend time in the church to explore some of its ancient ruins (such as the original baptismal font which dates back to the thirteenth century). A comfortable guesthouse, which can accommodate up to thirty people, is located on the monastery grounds.

POLAND

✠

Klasztor Zwiastowania

Biskupów 72
48-355 Burgabrice
Tel/Fax: (077) 439-82-06
E-mail: benedyktyni@nysa.com.pl

Founded in 1987, the Abbey of Zwiastowania is home to a community of Benedictine monks. All visitors are welcome to attend religious services, including Mass and the Liturgy of the Hours. The abbey operates a guesthouse called *The House of Spiritual Excercises*, which can accommodate up to twenty people. Those who wish to stay overnight must come with a disposition to participate more fully in the prayer life of the monks.

Jasna Góra—Sanctuary of the Polish Nation
Monastery of the Pauline Fathers

ul. O. A. Kordeckiego 2
42225 Częstochowa
Tel: (034) 365-66-88 • Fax: (034) 365-67-28
E-mail: klasztor@jasnagora.pl,
sanktuarium@jasnagora.pl
information@jasnagora.pl
centrum.informacji@jasnagora.pl
Web Site: www.jasnagora.pl
Dom Pielgrzyma im. Jana Palwa II (Pilgrim's House)
Ul. Kard. Wyszyńskiego 1/31
42-225 Częstochowa 25
Tel: (034) 324-70-11
Fax: (034) 365-18-70
E-mail: dp@jasnagora.pl

Founded in 1383, the Cloister of Paulinów is home to a community of Pauline Fathers, who serve as custodians of one of Eastern Europe's most famous Marian Shrines—Our Lady of Częstoçhowa. As well as praying before the miraculous image of the Blessed Virgin Mary, visitors can attend the many daily religious services that take place in the renowned pilgrimage church. Some of the sanctuary's most popular feast days are May 3 (Virgin, Queen of Poland), August 15 (The Assumption), August 26 (Black Madonna), September 8 (Birth of the Blessed Virgin Mary), and the first Sunday of October (Our

Lady of the Rosary). The Pauline Fathers operate the Pilgrim's House, which has more than one hundred comfortable rooms as well as a restaurant. For more information about the shrine, please refer to my book, *Catholic Shrines of Central & Eastern Europe: A Pilgrim's Travel Guide* (published by Liguori Publications).

Klasztor Ojców Bernardynów

Ulica Bernadynska 46
34130 Kalwaria Zebrzydowska (Kraków)
Tel: (033) 87-66-304 • Fax: (033) 87-66-641

Founded in 1603, the Monastery of the Virgin of the Angels is home to a community of Bernardine Fathers, who serve as custodians of Poland's second most famous shrine—Kalwaria Zebrzydowska. A dynamic place of pilgrimage, the monastery is home to numer-

ous celebrations, processions, and daily religious activities. One of the most prominent sites is the Zebrzydowski Chapel with its miraculous painting of the Blessed Virgin. Often referred to as the "Polish Jerusalem," the sanctuary is known for its annual Passion plays. The site remains Pope John Paul's favorite boyhood shrine: he grew up just five miles from here. The monastery operates a guesthouse, which welcomes both individuals and groups.

Opactwo Benedyktynów

Ul. Benedyktynska 37
30-375 Kraków-Tyniec
Tel: (012) 2675-526, 2675-977 • Fax: (012) 2619-000
Web Site: http://sklep.tyniec.mm.com.pl

According to local tradition, King Casimir founded the Abbey of Tyniec in 1044, which is now home to a community of Benedictine monks. Visitors are welcome to visit the abbey and participate in the monastic religious services, including Mass and the Liturgy of the

Hours. Vespers and the Sunday Mass are sung in Gregorian chant. Guest rooms can accommodate thirty-five individuals, mostly men, but mixed groups may also be accepted. Polish, English, German, French, Italian, and Russian are spoken at the abbey. The monastery operates a small gift shop, as well as a publishing house.

Sanktuarium Bożego Milosierdzia— Shrine of Divine Mercy

ul. Siostry Faustyny 3
30-420 Kraków-Łagiewniki
Tel: (012) 266-58-59, 267-61-04 • Fax: (012) 267-61-04, 266-23-68
E-mail:webmast@sanktuarium.krakow.pl
Web Site: http://www.sanktuarium.krakow.pl/english/e_index.html

Home to a community of the Sisters of Mercy, this convent is the site where Christ appeared to Saint Faustina between the years 1931 and 1938, entrusting her with the mission to spread devotion to his divine Mercy. Today, the shrine welcomes pilgrims and visitors throughout the year who come to pray at the renowned sanctuary. The largest crowds arrive on the first Sunday after Easter, which is the Feast of the Divine Mercy. The sisters operate a guesthouse for those men and women who are seeking a place of spiritual refreshment and solitude. Reservations must be made well in advance.

Klasztor Karmelitow Bosych

Ulica Swietoduska 14
20082 Lublin
Tel: (081) 53-202-44
Fax: (081) 53-444-60
E-mail: wsdlublin@karmel.pl

Founded in 1624, the Cloister of Bosych is home to a community of Carmelite monks. Visitors are welcome to attend daily Mass in the abbey church, as well as the sacred music concerts that are held throughout the year. Guest rooms are available to those men who wish to participate in a personal retreat of prayer and silence. You may purchase Gregorian chant and other sacred music tapes at the abbey.

Klasztor Ojców Franciszkanów

Niepokalanów
96-515 Teresin k. Sochaczewa
Tel: (046) 861-37-01 • Fax: (046) 861-37-59
E-mail:wof@niepokalanow.pl
Web Site: http://www.niepokalanow.pl

Founded in the late 1920s by Saint Maximilian Kolbe, the small town and friary of Niepokalanów is home to a community of Franciscan friars. Open throughout the year, the shrine has many activities and exhibits related to the life of its founder who died a martyr at Auschwitz. As well as attending religious services with the friars, pilgrims and tourists can visit the shrine's museum, Saint Maximilian's first room, the statue of the Immaculata (the first object placed on the soil in 1927), and a puppet show depicting the history of Christianity in Poland. The friars operate two large guesthouses, which provide accommodation for approximately one hundred and eighty people.

Casa das Irmas dominicanas

Rua Francisco Marto 50
2495 Fatima
Tel: (0249) 533-317 • Fax: (0249) 532-688

Founded during the twentieth century, the convent is home to a community of Dominican nuns. Located near Our Lady of Fátima, the famous Marian shrine, the convent operates a guesthouse which provides hospitality and overnight accommodation to those pilgrims who come to pray at the site where, in 1917, the Blessed Virgin Mary appeared to three small children. Serving as a very comfortable and well-organized guesthouse, the Casa das Irmas Dominicanas has more than forty rooms that are available to both individuals and groups. An excellent restaurant is located on the premises. All guests are welcome to join the nuns in religious services, including Mass, the Liturgy of the Hours, and the rosary.

Convento de Sao Francisco

Rua dos Mártires 1
2400 Leiria
Tel: (0244) 32754

Founded in 1902, the Convent of Saint Francis is home to a community of Franciscan Minors. All visitors can participate in religious services, which include Mass and the Liturgy of the Hours. Two of the most important feast days celebrated at the chapel are those honoring Saint Anthony (June 13) and Saint Francis (October 4). The friars operate a very large hotel, which welcomes individuals, families, and groups for prayer and reflection.

Santuário e Convento Nossa Senhora de Balsamao

Balsamao-Macedo de Cavaleiros
5340-091 Chacim
Tel: (0278) 468010 • Fax: (0278) 468028

Founded in the seventeenth century, the convent of Nossa Senhora de Balsamao is now home to a community of Marian Fathers, who serve as custodians of the famous Marian shrine located here. As well as attending the convent's religious services, the faithful can pray before the shrine's miraculous image of the Blessed Virgin Mary. The fathers operate a well-established guesthouse which has thirty-five rooms and an excellent restaurant.

Mosteiro de Santa Escolastica

4795-311 Roriz (Santo Tirso-Porto)
Tel: (0252) 941-232, 871-655 • Fax: (0252) 881-525

Founded in 1938, the Monastery of Santa Escolastica is home to a community of Benedictine monks. All visitors are welcome to join the monks in daily religious services, including Mass and Vespers. Thirteen guest rooms are available to families and young people. Everyone is invited to purchase the monks' famous "homemade" chocolates.

SCOTLAND

Sancta Maria Abbey

Nunraw, Garvald
East Lothian EH41 4LW
Tel: (01620) 830-223, 83-228 • Fax: (01620) 830-304
Web Site: http://liamdevlin.tripod.com/nunraw/abbey.htm

Founded in 1946, Sancta Maria Abbey is the thriving home of the Cistercian monks in Scotland, and one of the three principal abbeys belonging to the order in Great Britain. As well as daily prayer, the monks devote their time to raising cattle in order to finance the monastery. The guesthouse accommodates approximately thirty people, all are encouraged to participate in the prayer life of the monks.

Pluscarden Abbey

The Guestmaster
St. Benedict's or St. Scholastica's Retreat
Elgin, Morayshire IV30 3UA
Fax: (01343) 890-258
Web Site: www.pluscardenabbey.org

Founded in 1230, today Pluscarden Abbey is home to a community of twenty-seven Benedictine monks. Offering an authentic monastic experience, visitors are welcome to attend the monks' Mass and Liturgy of the Hours, which are sung in Gregorian chant. Women are housed in St. Scholastica's Retreat House (twelve comfortable bedrooms with modern facilities), while men are housed in the newly built wing of the abbey (fourteen bedrooms). Guests are invited to share lunch and supper with the monks in the refectory. The abbey gift shop carries a variety of books, gifts, souvenirs, as well as honey from the monks' apiary, bees-wax polish, and fresh fruit from their garden. Gregorian chant CDs and cassette tapes of the Pluscarden monks are available, both at the gift shop and over the Internet (visit their Web site).

SPAIN

Monasterio Santa María las Huelgas

Las Huelgas
09001 Burgos
Tel: (0947) 201-630, 206-045 • Fax: (0947) 273-686
E-mail: ocsosmrlh@planalfa.es
Web Site: http://www3.planalfa.es/lashuelgas

Founded in 1187, the Monastery of Santa María las Huelgas is home to a community of Cistercian monks. Mass is celebrated daily. The most important feast days at the abbey are those honoring Our Lady of Mount Carmel (July 17) and Saint Elie (July 20). Only women can be accommodated at the guesthouse.

Monasterio San Pedro de Cardeña

09193 Castrillo del Val (Burgos)
Tel: (0947) 290-033 • Fax: (0947) 290-075
E-mail: ocsocardena@planalfa.es

Founded in 899, the Monastery of San Pedro de Cardeña is home to a community of Cistercian monks. The faithful are welcome to join the monks in their prayer life of Mass and the Liturgy of the Hours. Only men can be accommodated at the guesthouse.

Monasterio de San Jerónimo de Yuste
10430 Cuacos de la Vera (Cáceres)
Tel: (0927) 172-130

Founded in 1408, the
Monastery of San Jerónimo de
Yuste is home to a small
community of Spanish monks.
When touring the abbey
grounds, you can visit the
monastery cloister, refectory,
and attend Mass in the Gothic

church. Since the guesthouse has just four rooms, only men can be
accommodated for an overnight stay.

Monasterio de Santa María del Parral
Subida del Parral 2
40003 Segovia
Tel: (0921) 43-12-98 • Fax: (0921) 42-25-92

Founded in 1454, the Monastery of Santa María del Parral is home to a
community of Herminite monks. All visitors are welcome to tour parts of
the abbey, which was declared a national monument in 1914. Mass is chanted
in the chapel daily. The most important feast days celebrated at the abbey
are September 8 (Saint Mary of Parral) and September 30 (Saint Jerome).
Only men can be accommodated in the twenty-three room guesthouse.

Real Monasterio de Santa María de El Paular
28741 El Paular (Rascafría)
Tel: (091) 869-1425

Founded in 1153, the Monastery of Santa María de El Paular is home to
a community of Benedictine monks. As well as touring the abbey and
surrounding area, visitors are welcome to attend the abbey's Mass, which is
sung in Gregorian chant. Although the monastery can only accommodate
men, there is a hotel nearby which can provide excellent accommodations.
You can contact them at: Santa María de El Paular, Tel: (091) 869-1011, Fax:
(091) 869-1006.

Monasterio de San Benito

31200 Estella (Navarra)
Tel: (0948) 550-882

Founded in 1616, the Monastery of San Benito is home to a community of Benedictine monks. Both the monastery's celebration of Mass and the Liturgy of the Hours are open to the public. Guest rooms are available to accommodate those individuals who wish to embark on a monastic retreat of prayer and silence. Several different cassettes of the monks' recorded music can be purchased at the monastery.

Monasterio de Nuestra Señora del Olivar

44558 Estercuel (Teruel)
Tel: (0978) 72-70-09, 75-23-00
E-mail: elolivar@arrakis.es
Web Site: www.arrakis.es/~elolivar

Founded in the early thirteenth century, the Monastery of the Virgin of the Olive Grove is home to a famous Marian shrine and miraculous statue. According to legend, a small hermitage was first built at the site where a wooden statue of the Virgin Mary was discovered. As the popularity of the image grew, the Order of Mercy Friars were invited to act as custodians of the newly established shrine. Today, the monastery serves not only as the novitiate and training house for the Order of Mercy Friars but also as a pilgrimage site. Visitors are welcome to join in the prayer life of the monks. Annually, on September 24, the abbey attracts thousands of pilgrims when the shrine celebrates the Feast of Our Lady of Mercy. A guesthouse with twenty-three rooms is available to accommodate visiting pilgrims (open to men, women, and children).

Padre Hospedero

Monasterio de Santa María de la Vid
Ctra. De Soria, s/n.
09491 La Vid de Aranda (Burgos)
Tel: (0947) 530-510, 530-051-4 • Fax: (0947) 530-429
E-mail: licet@mx3.redestb.es
Web Site: http://personal.redestb.es/licet/hosped.htm

Founded in 1162, the Monastery of Santa María de la Vid is home to a community of Augustinian monks. As well as participating in religious services in the abbey, visitors can tour the church, cloister, "funeral chapel," refectory, library, and the ancient hotel that was used for pilgrims who were traveling to Santiago de Compostela. A guesthouse with fifty-four rooms provides accommodation to both men and women who are seeking a time of spiritual refreshment in a monastic environment. Annually, on June 1, a large Marian procession is held at the abbey.

Monasterio de Santa Teresa de Ávila

20210 Lazkao (Gipuzkoa)
Tel: (0943) 88-01-70 • Fax: (0943) 16-08-68
E-mail: benedictinos@euskalnet.net

Founded in 1640, the Monastery of Santa Teresa de Ávila is home to a community of Benedictine monks. Mass is celebrated daily in the abbey chapel, which all are invited to attend. Those who wish to participate more fully in the prayer life of the community can ask to be accommodated in one of the monastery guest rooms (there are twenty rooms for men, eight for families).

Monasterio Nuestra Señora del Espino

Santa Gadea del Cid.
09200 Miranda de Ebro (Burgos)
Tel: (0947) 35-90-15

Originally founded in 1443, the Monastery of Nuestra Señora del Espino is home to a community of Redemptorist Fathers. As well as touring the vast abbey church, visitors can participate in religious services with the community. Only groups can be accommodated in the guesthouse, which is located inside the monastery. There is another hotel located at the exterior of the monastery which accepts young people.

Convento-Santuário de Nuestra Señora de Montesclaros

39417 Montesclaros (Santander)
Tel: (0942) 770-559, 770-553

Founded in the sixteenth century, the convent and shrine of Nuestra Señora de Montesclaros is home to a community of Dominicans monks. A popular pilgrimage site, the monastic sanctuary has a miraculous image of the Blessed Virgin Mary that dates back to the eighth century. As well as attending the many processions and celebrations that are held at the shrine annually, the faithful can also participate in daily religious services in the chapel. A guesthouse with forty rooms is available to pilgrims and retreat participants.

Despatx de la Basilica

08199 Montserrat
Tel: (093) 877.77.66 (ext. 1503) • Fax: (093) 877.77.50
Booking & Information Office:
Tel: (093) 877.77.01 • Fax: (093) 877.77.24
E-mail: serveidepremsa@abadiamontserrat.net
Web Site: www.abadiamontserrat.net

Founded in the eleventh century, the renowned abbey and sanctuary of Our Lady of Montserrat is home to a community of Benedictine monks. For centuries, this monastery has served as one of Europe's most important places of pilgrimage since, within its walls, it possesses a twelfth-century miraculous statue of the Blessed Virgin Mary. One million pilgrims and visitors travel here annually not only to pray before the beloved image but also to hear one of the country's oldest and most famous boys' choirs—the Escolania. As well as the activities associated with the shrine, visitors are invited to attend the Liturgy of the Hours and Mass with the monks in the abbey church. Since the monastery offers several types of accommodation, it is best to contact them in advance to make reservations (or visit their Web site).

Monasterio de San Benet

08199 Montserrat (Barcelona)
Tel: (093) 83-50-078
E-mail: stbenet@nexo.es

Founded in 1954, the Monastery of San Benet is home to a community of Benedictine monks. Mass is celebrated daily. Many pilgrims visit the abbey for the two feast days of Saint Benedict (March 21 and July 11). Only women can be accommodated in the monastery guesthouse, which has eight rooms.

Monasterio de Oseira

32135 Oseira (Ourense)
Tel: (0988) 282-804, 282-004 • Fax: (0988) 282-528

Founded in 1137, the Monastery of Oseira is home to a community of Cistercian monks. As well as visiting the abbey church, the faithful can join the monks for the daily celebration of Mass and the Liturgy of the Hours. Four-teen guest rooms are available  to those men and women who wish to embark on a monastic retreat of prayer and silence. Meals are shared with the monks in the refectory.

Monasterio de San Pelayo

Calle San Vicente 11
33003 Oviedo (Principado de Asturias)
Tel: (098) 521-89-81
E-mail: mspelayo@las.es

Founded in the ninth century, the Monastery of San Pelayo is home to a community of Benedictine monks. Only women and couples can be accommodated in the abbey guesthouse, which has six rooms. Mass is celebrated daily in the chapel with chant.

Monasterio de San Salvado

09132 Palacios de Benaver (Burgos)
Tel: (0947) 45-02-09 • Fax: (0947) 45-02-62

Founded in 834, the Monastery of San Salvador is home to a community of Benedictine monks. As well as praying in the chapel, visitors can attend Mass and the Liturgy of the Hours, which are sung in Gregorian chant. The guesthouse, which has nine rooms, provides accommodation to those men and women who wish to participate more fully in the prayer life of the monks. Meals are eaten with the monks which enriches your visit to the monastery.

Monasterio de Santa María la Real y San Bernardo

Camino de la Real 3
07010 Palma de Mallorca
Tel: (0971) 75-04-95 • Fax: (0971) 76-44-12

Founded in 1232, the Monastery of Santa María la Real y San Bernardo is home to a community of Missionary Fathers of the Sacred Heart. Although people come throughout the year, the most popular day is August 20 (the feast day of Saint Bernard), when numerous celebrations take place. Both men and women (traveling independently or in groups) are welcome to remain for a short stay in the abbey guesthouse, which has twenty-six rooms.

Convento–Santuario de Nuestra Señora de Cura
07629 Randa (Mallorca)
Tel: (0971) 66-09-94 • Fax: (0971) 66-20-52

Founded in the twelfth century, the convent and sanctuary of Our Lady of Cura is home to a community of Franciscan friars. As well as enjoying the beautiful panoramic view of the surrounding countryside, the faithful can spend personal time in the chapel (which is filled with Baroque statues), visit the library-museum, and attend religious services. A guesthouse with twenty-five rooms provides accommodation for both men and women.

Abadía de Roncesvalles (Abbaye de Roncevaux)
31650 Roncesvalles (PA)
Tel: (0948) 76-00-00 • Tel (Guesthouse): (0948) 76-02-25
Fax: (0948) 79-04-50

Founded in 1127, the Abbey of Roncesvalles is home to a community of Canons Regular. As well as touring the ancient church, visitors can join the monks in their celebration of Mass. A guesthouse is available to those individuals who wish to spend personal time in retreat.

Monasterio de San Julián de Samos
27620 Samos (Lugo)
Tel: (0982) 54-60-46 • Fax: (0982) 54-61-82

Originally founded in the sixth century, the Monastery of San Julián de Samos is now home to a community of Benedictine monks. Mass is celebrated daily. The most important feast days celebrated at the monastery are those honoring Saint Julian (January 9) and Saint Benedict (March 21 and July 11). Forty guest rooms are available to those individuals who wish to participate more fully in the prayer life of the community. Organ concerts are held at certain times of the year.

Monasterio de Santa María de Huerta
42260 Santa María de Huerta (Soria)
Tel: (0975) 327-002 • Fax: (0975) 327-397

Founded in 1162, the Monastery of Santa María de Huerta is home to a community of Cistercian monks. Visitors can tour parts of the abbey as well as take part in religious services with the monks. Twelve guest rooms are available to those individuals who seek a place for prayer and silence and who wish to experience monastic life firsthand. Items available at the abbey gift shop include its own cheese, wine, meat, honey, books, and the liquor called "Tizona."

Hospedería
"Maison d'Accueil Spirituel"
09610 Santo Domingo de Silos
Tel: (0947) 39-00-68, 39-00-49 • Fax: (0947) 39-00-33

Located in north-central Spain, the monastery of Santo Domingo de Silos is home to a community of Benedictine monks. In the mid 1990s, this abbey gained international fame for their recordings of Gregorian chant which "hit number one" on the European pop charts, as well as making a great impression in the United States. Pilgrims and visitors are invited to attend religious services with the monks, which include a morning High Mass and singing the canonical hours. Guided tours of the abbey are also available. A guesthouse (Hospedería) is located next to the monastery, providing accommodation to both men and women.

Monasterio San Juan de la Cruz

Alameda de la Fuencisla
40003 Segovia
Tel: (0921) 43-13-49, 43-19-61 • Fax: (0921) 43-16-50

Founded in 1586, the Monastery of San Juan de la Cruz is now home to a community of Carmelite monks. Pilgrims come throughout the year to pray before the relics of the great mystic, Saint John of the Cross. As well as visiting the museum which is dedicated to the life of the saint, the faithful are invited to join the Carmelites for Mass in the chapel. A guesthouse with forty rooms provides accommodation to both men and women.

Monasterio Casa de la Trinidad

39150 Suesa (Santander)

Founded in 1887, the monastery is home to a community of Holy Trinity monks. Everyone is welcome to attend religious services with the monks, which include Mass and the Liturgy of the Hours. The fourteen-room guesthouse can accommodate up to thirty-five people.

Monasterio Santa María de la Caridad

31522 Tulebras (Navarra)
Tel: (0948) 851-475 • Fax: (0948) 850-012
E-mail: ocsocari@planalfa.es

Founded in 1147, the Monastery of Santa Maria de la Caridad is home to a community of Cistercian monks. As well as exploring the abbey church and museum, visitors are invited to attend the daily celebration of Mass with the monks. Only those men and women who seek to participate more fully in the prayer life of the monks can be accepted for an overnight stay in the small guesthouse.

Abadía de Santa Cruz del Valle de los Caídos

Valle de Los Caídos
28029 Valle de Los caídos (Madrid)
Tel: (091) 890-5411 • Fax: (091) 890-5594
E-mail: abadia-valle@ctv.es

Founded in 1958, the Abbey of Santa Cruz del Valle de los Caídos is home to a community of Benedictine monks. All visitors are welcome to attend religious services, including the solemn High Mass which takes place every morning. Accommodation is available in either of the two separate guesthouses. In the guesthouse located inside the monastery, men can be accommodated in sixteen rooms. In the other guesthouse, which is located at the exterior, both men and women can be accommodated in one hundred and ten rooms. For further information about the latter, you may contact them by telephone (091) 890-5492 or fax (091) 896-1542.

Abadía de San Salvador de Leyre

31410 Yesa (Navarra)
Tel (Abbey): (0948) 884-011 • Fax (Abbey): (0948) 884-230
Tel (Guesthouse): (0948) 884-100 • Fax (Guesthouse): (0948) 884-137

Situated at the top of a mountain, offering spectacular views of the valley below, the Abbey of Saint Salvador of Leyre was founded in the ninth century and is now home to a community of Benedictine monks. Visitors can tour the abbey and attend religious services with the monks,  which include the singing of the Liturgy of the Hours and Mass in Gregorian chant. Twenty-nine guest rooms are available to both men and women who are either traveling independently or in groups.

Hospice du Grand-Saint-Bernard

1946 Bourg-Saint-Pierre
Tel: (027) 787-12-36 • Fax: (027) 787-11-07
Web Site: www.saint-bernard.ch

Founded by Saint Bernard of Menthon, the Grand-Saint-Bernard Hospice is home to a community of Benedictine monks who have provided food and shelter to pilgrim travelers at the Swiss-Italian border for almost a thousand years. Located high in the European Alps, this is where  the monks first bred Saint Bernard dogs, later training them to rescue stranded and lost travelers. Today, many pilgrims and groups still visit the hospice to share in the simple religious services with the monks and refresh themselves with the beautiful scenery of the Swiss Alps.

Monastère Saint-Joseph

1868 Collombey
Tel: (024) 471-23-69 • Fax: (024) 472-29-04

Founded in 1629, the Monastery of Saint-Joseph is home to a community of Bernardine monks. The monks celebrate Mass and the Liturgy of the Hours in the abbey chapel daily, which all visitors are invited to attend. Religious services are sung in both French and Gregorian chant. A guesthouse is available to both men and women with special accommodations for groups of young people. The major apostolic work of the monks includes making hosts, liturgical vestments, and chaplets.

Monastère du Carmel

2802 Develier
Tel: (032) 422-82-21 • Fax: (032) 422-82-24

Founded in 1946, this monastery is home to a community of Carmelites. The Mass and Liturgy of the Hours are celebrated in French, all visitors are welcome to attend religious services with the monks. There are only two guest rooms available to those individuals who seek a personal retreat of prayer and silence.

Kloster Einsiedeln

8840 Einsiedeln (Schwyz)
Tel: (055) 526-240 • Fax: (055) 418-61-12
E-mail (Abbey): einsiedeln@kath.ch
Web Site (Abbey): www.kath.ch/einsiedeln
E-mail (Tourist Office): info@einsiedeln.ch
Web Site (Tourist Office): www.einsiedeln.ch

Founded in 934, the Abbey of Einsiedeln is home to a community of Benedictine monks. Serving as one of Switzerland's most famous places of pilgrimage, the monastery is home to a miraculous image of the Blessed Virgin Mary, which is located in the Chapel of Our Lady. Down through the centuries, the abbey has retained its processions, solemn liturgies, and tradition of sacred music, with orchestral Masses still performed occasionally during the High Mass. Many religious services take place in the abbey church daily, including Mass, the Liturgy of the Hours, and the rosary. Most prayers are sung in Gregorian chant. The monks from this abbey have gained international attention for their sacred music. Guest rooms are available to individuals and groups who seek to spend a few days in prayerful retreat, however, one must reserve a room well in advance of their arrival. Close to the monastery, there are also a large number of bed-and-breakfast inns that can provide accommodations for both visitors and pilgrims.

Benedektiner Abtei
6390 Engelberg (Sarnem)
Tel: (041) 639-61-61 • Fax: (041) 630-61-13

Founded in 1120, the Abbey of Engelberg is home to a community of Benedictine monks. Guided tours of both the abbey and church are available, all visitors can participate in the prayer life of the monks, which includes Mass and the Liturgy of the Hours. Since the abbey has just a few guest rooms, only men can be accommodated.

Monastère Notre-Dame-de-l'Assomption
1470 Estavayer-le-Lac (Fribourg)
Tel: (026) 663-42-22 • Fax: (026) 663-54-39

Founded in 1280, the Monastery of Notre-Dame-de-l'Assomption is home to a women's community of Dominican monks. As well as exploring the abbey church, visitors can join the monks in religious services, including Mass and the Liturgy of the Hours, which are sung in French and Gregorian chant. In 1997, the monastery opened a new guesthouse which has fifteen rooms (six rooms with two beds, eight rooms with one bed, and one room with four beds). The guesthouse is closed in January.

Abbaye Notre-Dame-de-la-Maigrauge
2, chemin de l'Abbaye
1700 Fribourg
Tel: (026) 322-91-50 • Fax: (026) 322-91-55

Founded in 1284, the Abbey of Notre-Dame-de-la-Maigrauge is home to a community of Cistercian monks. Central to the life of the monks is the Mass and the Liturgy of the Hours, which are sung in French and Gregorian chant. A small guesthouse, renovated in 1997, provides accommodation for up to nine people who wish to embark on a personal retreat in a monastic environment.

Monastère Saint-Joseph-de-Montorge

Chemin de Lorette 10
1700 Fribourg
Tel: (026) 322-35-36 • Fax: (026) 322-35-58

Founded in 1628, the monastery is home to a women's community of Capuchin monks. The Liturgy of the Hours and Mass are said in French, all visitors are welcome to join the nuns in the abbey church for religious services. A small guesthouse provides accommodation only to women and young girls who wish to participate more fully in the prayer life of the monastery. The nuns' major apostolic work includes the production of liturgical vestments, as well as making hosts.

Monastère de la Visitation

16, rue de Morat
1700 Fribourg
Tel: (026) 347-23-40 • Fax: (026) 347-23-49

Founded in 1635, the Monastery of the Visitation is home to a women's community of the Visitation Order. Both Mass and the Liturgy of the Hours are celebrated in the abbey church, which all are invited to attend. The guesthouse is open only to women and young ladies who wish to join the nuns in their monastic life of prayer.

Monastère Sainte-Claire ("La Grand-Part")

Chemin des Crosettes 13
1805 Jongny (VD)
Tel: (021) 921-21-77 • Fax: (021) 922-07-35

Founded in 1424, the Monastery of Sainte-Clare is home to a community of Poor Clare nuns. All visitors are welcome to participate in the prayer life of the nuns, which includes the celebration of Mass and the Liturgy of the Hours in the chapel (recited in French). Individuals seeking a place for prayer and silence can ask to be accommodated in one of the abbey guest rooms.

Kloster Sankt Johann Baptist

7537 Müstair (Davos)
Tel: (082) 85-265

Founded in the ninth century, the Cloister of Saint John the Baptist is home to a community of Benedictine monks. As well as visiting the various historic chapels in the abbey church, pilgrims and tourists can attend religious services with the monks, which are open to the public. Since there are only six guest rooms available, only those men and women who are willing to participate in the prayer life of the monastery during their stay can be accommodated.

Abbaye d'Hauterive

1725 Posieux
Tel: (026) 402-17-83 • Fax: (026) 401-10-53

Founded in 1138, the Abbey of Hauterive is home to a community of Cistercian monks. Guided tours of the thirteenth and fourteenth church and cloister are available during the week, and also after High Mass on Sundays. Mass and the Liturgy of the Hours are sung in Gregorian chant, while the regular presentations given by the monks are in French. Seventeen guest rooms are available for men, six guest rooms for women, and a dormitory room with eight beds for groups of young people.

Monastero di Santa Maria Presentata

Via di Santa Maria ai Pioppi
7742 Poschiavo (Pontresina)
Tel: (081) 844-02-04 • Fax: (081) 844-32-11

Founded in 1629, the Monastery of Santa Maria Presentata is home to a women's community of Augustinian monks. In 1972, the ancient monastery was replaced by a more modern one. The most popular days at the abbey church are the feast days honoring Saint Bernard (August 20) and Saint Augustine (August 28). Since the nuns have just a few guest rooms, only women may be accommodated.

Abbaye de la Fille-Dieu

1680 Romont
Tel: (026) 652-22-42 • Fax: (026) 652-23-15
Web Site: www.fille-dieu.ch

Founded in 1268 by the Trappists, the Abbey of Fille-Dieu is now home to a women's community of Cistercian monks. In 1996, the monks reconsecrated the beautifully restored abbey church to honor the 650th anniversary of its original construction in 1346. Those visiting the monastery can attend Mass, which is sung in Gregorian chant, and the Liturgy of the Hours, which is sung in French. Individuals who wish to participate in a silent monastic retreat may be accommodated in one of the abbey's guest rooms.

Part 4

✠

Other European Places of Retreat

AS WELL AS being blessed with hundreds of monasteries and convents, Europe is also home to many other places of retreat. Listed below are a number of these places which offer both solitude and peace. Linked to many famous shrines and pilgrimage sites, these retreat houses are run by religious, laypeople, or a combination of both. (For a complete description of the shrines and pilgrimage sites near which they are located, please refer to my previous books: *Catholic Shrines of Western Europe* and *Catholic Shrines of Central & Eastern Europe*).

AUSTRIA

Haus Marillac
Sennstrasse 3
6020 Innsbruck
Tel: (0512) 572-313 • Fax: (0512) 572-313-10

Located near the pilgrimage church (and town) of Absam, which has a miraculous image of the Blessed Virgin Mary.

Haus Der Begegnung
Tschurtschentaler Strasse 2a
6020 Innsbruck
Tel: (0512) 587-869 • Fax: (0512) 587-869-11

Located near the pilgrimage church (and town) of Absam, which has a miraculous image of the Blessed Virgin Mary.

Barmherzige Schwestern
Schwester Pia Maria
Rennweg 40
6020 Innsbruck
Tel: (0512) 587-176-15

Located near the pilgrimage church (and town) of Absam, which has a miraculous image of the Blessed Virgin Mary.

Marienheim
Pater-Heinrich-Abel. Platz 3
8630 Mariazell
Tel: (03882) 25-45

Located near the shrine of Our Lady of Mariazell, the most popular Marian pilgrimage site in Central Europe.

Salvatorheim
Abt-Severin-Gasse 7
8630 Mariazell
Tel: (03882) 22-16-0 • Fax: (03882) 22-16-11

Located near the shrine of Our Lady of Mariazell, the most popular Marian pilgrimage site in Central Europe.

Kleine Schwestern Jesu
Dr. Lueger-Gasse 18
8630 Mariazell
Tel: (03882) 27-25

Located near the shrine of Our Lady of Mariazell, the most popular Marian pilgrimage site in Central Europe.

Herzmarien Karmel
Karmelweg 1
8630 Mariazell
Tel: (03882) 26-19

Located near the shrine of Our Lady of Mariazell, the most popular Marian pilgrimage site in Central Europe.

Haus Saint Franziskus
Heimweg 3
8630 Saint Sebastian-Mariazell
Tel: (03882) 60-23 • Fax: (2742) 844-180

Located near the shrine of Our Lady of Mariazell, the most popular Marian pilgrimage site in Central Europe.

Erzb. Priesterseminar
Dreifaltigkeitsgasse 14
Postfach 66
5024 Salzburg
Tel: (0662) 877-495, (0662) 877-495-0 • Fax: (0662) 877-495-62

Located near the pilgrimage sites of Our Lady of Maria Plain and the Christ Child of Loreto in Salzburg. Home to the Salzburg seminary, the Priesterseminar has fifty single and ten double guest rooms for both men and women.

Christkönigkolleg
Kapitelplatz 2a
A-5020 Salzburg
Tel: (0662) 84-26-27

Located near the pilgrimage sites of Our Lady of Maria Plain and the Christ Child of Loreto in Salzburg. Accommodations of sixteen beds are available from July to September, which is reduced to eight beds during the academic year.

Johanesschlössl (Apostlehouse) of the Palatine
Mönchsberg 24, P.O. Box 501
5010 Salzburg
Tel: (0662) 84-65-43 (ext. 72 or 78) • Fax: (0662) 84-63-47-86

Located near the pilgrimage sites of Our Lady of Maria Plain and the Christ Child of Loreto in Salzburg. The guesthouse has twenty-five single rooms and ten double rooms.

Stephanushaus

Ungargasse 38
1030 Vienna
Tel: (1) 717-03 • Fax: (1) 717-03-812

Located near the pilgrimage sites of Our Lady of the Bowed Head and the Cathedral of Saint Stephen in Vienna. Operated by sisters, Saint Stephen's House provides excellent accommodation near the city center.

Hotel "Don Bosco"

Hagenmüllergasse 33
1030 Vienna
Tel: (1) 711-84-555, (1) 711-84-0 • Fax: (1) 711-84-112

Located near the pilgrimage sites of Our Lady of the Bowed Head and the Cathedral of Saint Stephen in Vienna. Open only between July and September, the Don Bosco Hotel offers excellent accommodations in a very pleasant atmosphere.

Kardinal-König-Haus

Lainzer Strasse 138
1130 Vienna
Tel: (1) 804-75-93 • Fax: (1) 804-97-43
E-mail: office@kardinal-koenig-haus.at
Web Site: www.kardinal-koenig-haus.at

Located near the pilgrimage sites of Our Lady of the Bowed Head and the Cathedral of Saint Stephen in Vienna.

Pallotti-Haus

Auhofstrasse 10
1130 Vienna
Tel: (1) 877-10-72 • Fax: (1) 877-10-72-29

Located near the pilgrimage sites of Our Lady of the Bowed Head and the Cathedral of Saint Stephen in Vienna.

Don Bosco Haus

Saint Veit-Gasse 25
1130 Vienna
Tel: (1) 878-39 • Fax: (1) 878-39-414
E-mail: donbosco@magnet.at
Web Site: www.donbosco.at

Located near the pilgrimage sites of Our Lady of the Bowed Head and the Cathedral of Saint Stephen in Vienna.

Marianneum

Hetzendorfer Strasse 117
1120 Vienna
Tel: (1) 804-33-01 • Fax: (1) 804-33-01-17

Located near the pilgrimage sites of Our Lady of the Bowed Head and the Cathedral of Saint Stephen in Vienna.

Marienheim der Schulbrüder

Anton-Böck-Gasse 20
1210 Vienna
Tel: (1) 291-25 • Fax: (1) 290-18-39
E-mail: wbschulbrueder@wirtschaftsbetriebe.at

Located near the pilgrimage sites of Our Lady of the Bowed Head and the Cathedral of Saint Stephen in Vienna.

Seminarzentrum Am Spiegeln

Meyrinkgasse 7–9
1230 Vienna
Tel/Fax: (1) 889-30-93
E-mail: AmSpiegeln@compuserve.com

Located near the pilgrimage sites of Our Lady of the Bowed Head and the Cathedral of Saint Stephen in Vienna.

Exerzitienhaus der Schwestern vom göttlichen Erlöser

Kaiserstrasse 23–25
1070 Vienna
Tel: (1) 523-41-81 • Fax: (1) 523-64-44-833

Located near the pilgrimage sites of Our Lady of the Bowed Head and the Cathedral of Saint Stephen in Vienna.

Katholisches Bildungshaus Schönstatt am Kahlenberg

1190 Vienna
Tel: (1) 320-13-07

Located near the pilgrimage sites of Our Lady of the Bowed Head and the Cathedral of Saint Stephen in Vienna.

BELGIUM

Chateau de Chaityfontaine

Chaityfontaine 8
4860 Pepinster
Tel: (04) 360-91-71 • Fax: (04) 360-91-73

Located near the shrine of Our Lady of Banneux, the site of a Church-approved Marian apparition dating back to the 1930s. The Chateau de Chaityfontaine provides very comfortable accommodations.

Communauté Saint–Jean

Rue de la Sapinière 50
4141 Banneux N.D.
Tel: (04) 360.01.20 • Fax: (04) 360.01.29

Located near the shrine of Our Lady of Banneux, the site of a Church-approved Marian apparition dating back to the 1930s.

Carrefour
Avenue J. Nusbaum, 21
4141 Banneux N.d.
Tel: (04) 360-81-84 • Fax: (04) 360-93-45

Located near the shrine of Our Lady of Banneux, the site of a Church-approved Marian apparition dating back to the 1930s.

Mater Dei
Rue de l'Esplanade, 12
4141 Banneux N.D
Tel: (04) 360-81-36

Located near the shrine of Our Lady of Banneux, the site of a Church-approved Marian apparition dating back to the 1930s.

Hôtel de l'Aubépine
27, route de Rochefort
5570 Beauraing
Tel: (082) 71-11-59 • Fax: (082) 71-33-54

Located across the street from the shrine of Our Lady of Beauraing, the site of a Church-approved Marian apparition dating back to the 1930s.

ENGLAND

+‖+
+‖+

Elmham House Accommodation

Pilgrim Bureau, Friday Market
Walsingham, Norfolk NR22 6EG
Tel: (01328) 82-02-17 • Fax: (01328) 82-10-87
E-mail: rcnatshrne@aol.com
Web Site: http://walsingham.org.uk

Home to the shrine of Our Lady of Walsingham, where the Blessed Virgin Mary appeared in 1061 and asked a young lady to build a replica of the Holy House of Nazareth in Walsingham.

FRANCE

+‖+
+‖+

La Providence

Rue des Ecoles
01480 Ars-sur-Formans
Tel: (0474) 00-71-65 • Fax: (0474) 08-10-79

Operated by the shrine of Saint-John-Marie-Vianney, the pilgrimage site where the saint lived and worked.

Maison Saint–Jean Accueil

Allée Abbé-Nodet
01480 Ars-sur-Formans
Tel: (0474) 00-73-13 • Fax: (0474) 08-11-76

Operated by the shrine of Saint-John-Marie-Vianney, the pilgrimage site where the saint lived and worked.

Foyer Sacerdotal Jean–Paul II
Chemin de la Percellière
01480 Ars-sur-Formans
Tel: (0474) 08-19-00 • Fax: (0474) 08-19-08

Accommodation for priests and seminarians only, it is located near the shrine of Saint-John-Marie-Vianney, the pilgrimage site where the saint lived and worked.

Diocesan House
Maison Saint-Yves
1 rue Saint-Eman
28000 Chartres
Tel: (0237) 88.37.40 • Fax: (0237) 88.37.49

Located next to the world-famous Chartres Cathedral.

Foyer of the Holy Family
Quartier Notre-Dame
83570 Cotignac
Tel: (0494) 04-65-28

Located near the shrine of Saint Joseph, the pilgrimage site where the saint appeared to a shepherd in 1660.

Sanctuary of Our Lady of La Salette
38970 La Salette
Tel: (0476) 30-00-11 • Fax: (0476) 30-03-65
E-mail: infos@nd-la-salettee.com
Web Site: www.nd-la-salette.com

Home to the Church-approved Marian apparition site where the Virgin Mary appeared to two small children in 1846. Located at the top of the Alps, the shrine operates a very large retreat house, with accommodations ranging from dormitory bunks to hotellike rooms.

Ermitage of Saint Thérèse of Lisieux

23, rue du Carmel
14100 Lisieux
Tel: (0231) 48-55-10 • Fax: (0231) 48-55-27
E-mail: ermitage-ste-therese@therese-de-lisieux.com
Web Site: www.therese-de-lisieux.com

Located near the shrine and home of Saint Thérèse of Lisieux.

Foyer Louis and Zélie Martin

15, avenue Sainte-Thérèse
Tel: (0231) 62-09-33 • Fax: (0231) 62-88-65
E-mail: foyer-martin@therese-de-liseux.com
Web Site: www.therese-de-lisieux.com

Located near the shrine and home of Saint Thérèse of Lisieux.

Monastery of the Dominicans

Route de Pontacq
65100 Lourdes
Tel: (0562) 46.33.30 • Fax: (0562) 94-89-76

Located near the world-famous shrine of Our Lady of Lourdes, where, in 1858, the Blessed Virgin Mary appeared to Saint Bernadette.

Foyer Familial

Dominican Sisters of the Presentation
2, avenue Saint-Joseph
65100 Lourdes
Tel: (0562) 94-07-51 • Fax: (0562) 94-57-14

Located near the world-famous shrine of Our Lady of Lourdes, where, in 1858, the Blessed Virgin Mary appeared to Saint Bernadette.

Convent of the Immaculate Conception

4 bis, route de la Foret
65100 Lourdes
Tel: (0562) 94-20-22 • Fax: (0562) 94-93-19

Located near the world-famous shrine of Our Lady of Lourdes, where, in 1858, the Blessed Virgin Mary appeared to Saint Bernadette.

Sisters of the Love of God

17, rue de Bagnères
65100 Lourdes
Tel: (0562) 94-38-83 • Fax: (0562) 42-22-50

Located near the world-famous shrine of Our Lady of Lourdes, where, in 1858, the Blessed Virgin Mary appeared to Saint Bernadette.

Saint Thérèse House

32–24, rue du Sacré-Coeur
65100 Lourdes
Tel: (0562) 94-35-16 • Fax: (0562) 94-70-13

Located near the world-famous shrine of Our Lady of Lourdes, where, in 1858, the Blessed Virgin Mary appeared to Saint Bernadette.

Saint Gildard Convent

34, rue Saint-Gildard
58000 Nevers
Tel: (0386) 71-99-50 • Fax: (0386) 71-99-51

The chapel containing the incorrupt body of Saint Bernadette, housed in a glass reliquary, is located on the grounds of the Saint Gildard convent and shrine.

Couvent du Mont-Saint-Odile

67530 Ottrott
Tel: (3) 88-95-80-53 • Fax: (3) 88-95-82-96

Provides a very comfortable place of spiritual retreat for both men and women.

Maison du Sacré-Coeur

3 ter, rue de la Paix
71600 Paray-le-Monial
Tel: (0385) 81-05-43 • Fax: (0385) 81-68-08
E-mail: maisondusacrecoeurmsc@minitel.net

Located near the shrine and Chapel of the Visitation, the site where Jesus revealed his Sacred Heart to Saint Margaret Mary Alacoque in a number of apparitions between 1673 and 1675.

Foyer Nazareth

10, avenue de Charolles
71600 Paray-le-Monial
Tel: (0385) 81-11-88 • Fax: (0385) 81-56-19

Located near the shrine and Chapel of the Visitation, the site where Jesus revealed his Sacred Heart to Saint Margaret Mary Alacoque in a number of apparitions between 1673 and 1675.

Cor Christi Association, Foyer of the Sacred Heart

14, rue de la Visitation
71600 Paray-le-Monial
Tel: (0385) 81-11-01 • Fax: (0385) 81-26-83
E-mail: foyersc@club-internet.fr
Web Site: www.chez.com/fsc

Located near the shrine and Chapel of the Visitation, the site where Jesus revealed his Sacred Heart to Saint Margaret Mary Alacoque in a number of apparitions between 1673 and 1675.

Foyer Friedland

23, avenue de Friedland
75008 Paris
Tel: (0140) 76-30-30 • Fax: (0140) 76-30-00

Located in Paris, the home of the shrine of Our Lady of the Miraculous Medal, where, in 1830, the Blessed Virgin Mary appeared to Saint Catherine Labouré.

Maison Nicolas-Barré

83, rue de Sèvres
75006 Paris
Tel: (0145) 48-25-48 • Fax: (0142) 84-07-85

Located in Paris, the home of the shrine of Our Lady of the Miraculous Medal, where, in 1830, the Blessed Virgin Mary appeared to Saint Catherine Labouré.

Saint-Jean-Eudes

1, rue Jean Dolent
75014 Paris
Tel: (0144) 08-70-00 • Fax: (0143) 36 72-03

Located in Paris, the home of the shrine of Our Lady of the Miraculous Medal, where, in 1830, the Blessed Virgin Mary appeared to Saint Catherine Labouré. Reserved for priests, seminarians, religious, and laypeople who work for the Catholic Church.

Foyer M.-Mignard

2, villa de la Réunion
75016 Paris
Tel: (0145) 27-29-84 • Fax: (0145) 27-16-63

Located in Paris, the home of the shrine of Our Lady of the Miraculous Medal, where, in 1830, the Blessed Virgin Mary appeared to Saint Catherine Labouré.

M.C. Holy Family

46, rue de Montreuil
75011 Paris
Tel: (0143) 72-49-30

Located in Paris, the home of the shrine of Our Lady of the Miraculous Medal, where, in 1830, the Blessed Virgin Mary appeared to Saint Catherine Labouré.

Centre Eugénie–Milert

17, rue de l'Assomption
75018 Paris
Tel: (0146) 47-84-56 • Fax: (0142) 24-04-90

Located in Paris, the home of the shrine of Our Lady of the Miraculous Medal, where, in 1830, the Blessed Virgin Mary appeared to Saint Catherine Labouré.

Sanctuary of Our Lady of Mercy

Center for Pilgrimages
B.P. 7
36180 Pellevoisin
Tel: (0254) 39.06.49 • Fax: (0254) 39.04.66

Home to the shrine of Our Lady of Pellevoisin, the pilgrimage site where, in 1876, the Blessed Virgin Mary appeared and revealed the devotion to the Sacred Heart Scapular.

Fraternité Marie–Estelle

2, rue des Combattants en A.F.N.
36180 Pellevoisin
Tel: (0254) 39-03-02

Located near the shrine of Our Lady of Pellevoisin, the pilgrimage site where, in 1876, the Blessed Virgin Mary appeared and revealed the devotion to the Sacred Heart Scapular.

Centre Pastoral du Sanctuaire

3, rue Notre-Dame
53220 Pontmain
Tel: (0243) 05-07-60 • Fax: (0243) 05-08-32

Home to the shrine of Our Lady of Pontmain, the pilgrimage site where, in 1871, the Blessed Virgin Mary appeared to four small children.

Relais le Bocage

2, rue Mausson
53220 Pontmain
Tel: (0243) 05-08-81 • Fax: (0243) 05-01-54
Web Site: www.relais-le-bocage.com

Located near the shrine of Our Lady of Pontmain, the pilgrimage site where, in 1871, the Blessed Virgin Mary appeared to four small children.

L'Auberge de l'Espérance

9, rue de la Grange
53220 Pontmain
Tel: (0243) 05-08-10 • Fax: (0243) 05-03-19

Located near the shrine of Our Lady of Pontmain, the pilgrimage site where, in 1871, the Blessed Virgin Mary appeared to four small children.

Maison Saint-François

Rue Saint-Mayol
43000 Le Puy-en-Val
Tel: (0471) 05-98-86 • Fax: (0471) 05-98-87

Located near the famous Marian pilgrimage site of Our Lady of Le Puy.

Dominican Fathers
Hôtellerie de la Sainte-Baume
La Sainte-Baume
83640 Le Plan d'Aups-Sainte-Baume
Tel: (0442) 04-54-84 • Fax: (0442) 62-55-56

Home to the shrine of Saint Mary Magdalene, the cliffside grotto and pilgrimage site contains her relics.

Notre Dame Centre and Marie's Guest House
46500 Rocamadour
Tel: (0565) 33-23-23 • Fax: (0565) 33-23-24

Located near the pilgrimage shrine of Our Lady of Rocamadour. Advance reservations are absolutely necessary.

L'Abbaye
B.P. 1
22750 Saint-Jacut-de-la-Mer
Tel: (0296) 27-71-19 • Fax: (0296) 27-79-45
E-mail: abbaye.Saintjacut@wanadoo.fr
Web Site: http://perso.wanadoo.fr/abbaye.st.jacut

House of the Montfort Missionaries
4, rue Jean-Paul II – B.P. 45
85292 Saint-Laurent-sur-Sèvre Cédex
Tel: (0251) 64-37-00 • Fax: (0251) 67-87-34

Home to the shrine of Saint Louis de Montfort and the headquarters for the Montfort Missionaries.

GERMANY

August Pieper Haus
Leonhardstrasse 18–20
52064 Aachen
Tel: (0241) 47-99-60 • Fax: (0241) 47-99-610
Web Site: www.bistum-aachen.de

Located in the same city as the renowned Cathedral of Aachen.

Haus Eich
Jugenbildunghaus des
Bistums Aachen
Eupener Strasse 138
52066 Aachen
Tel: (0241) 60-92-0 • Fax: (0241) 60-92-660

Located in the same city as the renowned Cathedral of Aachen.

Dominikanerkloster Heilig Kreuz
Lindenstr. 45
D-50674 Köln
Tel: (0221) 207-140 • Fax: (0221) 207-1455
E-mail: nc-mertenma2@netcologne.de

Located in the same city as the famous Cathedral of Cologne.

Priesterseminar
Kardinal-Frings-Str. 12
D-50668 Köln
Tel: (0221) 16003-0 • Fax: (0221) 16003-410
Web Site: www.priesterseminar.de

Located in the same city as the famous Cathedral of Cologne. The
Priesterseminar is the Archdiocese of Cologne's seminary, which provides
very nice guest rooms for both men and women.

Collegium Albertinum

Adenauerallee 19
D-53111 Bonn
Tel: (0228) 2674-0 • Fax: (0228) 2674-182
E-mail: albertinum-sekretariat@gmx.de

Located in the same city as the famous Cathedral of Cologne. The Collegium Albertinum is a seminary in the Archdiocese of Bonn, which provides guest rooms for men.

Saint Pantaleons–Kloster

Am Pantaleonsberg 10
50676 Köln
Tel: (0221) 31-47-15

Located in the same city as the famous Cathedral of Cologne.

Tagungs—und Gästehaus Saint Georg

Rolandstrasse 61
50667 Köln
Tel: (0221) 93-70-20-0 • Fax: (0221) 93-70-20-44
E-mail: gaestehaus.st.georg@t-online.de

Located in the same city as the famous Cathedral of Cologne.

Kolping–Erwachsenens–Bildungswerk

Kolping Akademie
Diozesanverband München und Freising e.V.
Adolf-Kolping-Str. 1
80336 München
Tel: (085) 55-158-167 • Fax: (085) 55-158-165
E-mail: service@kolping-akademie-muenchen.de
Web Site: www.kolping-akademie-muenchen.de

Located in the popular city of Munich. Accommodation available for both individuals and groups.

Saint Pius-Kolleg

Der Steyler Missionare
Dauthendeystr. 25
81377 München
Tel: (089) 71-020

Located in the popular city of Munich. Accommodation usually reserved only for groups.

Vinzenz-Pallotti-Haus

Pallottinerstr. 2
Pf. 1741
85317 Freising
Tel: (08161) 96-890

Located just north of the city of Munich. Accommodation usually reserved only for groups.

Priesterhaus

Kapellenplatz 35
D-47623 Kevelaer
Tel: (02832) 93-380 • Fax: (02832) 70-726
E-mail: WallfahrtsleitungKevelaer@t-online.de
Web Sites: www.kevelaer.de

Located near the shrine of Our Lady of Kevelaer, one of Germany's two most popular Marian pilgrimage sites. The Priesterhaus provides housing only to pilgrimage groups, not to individuals.

HUNGARY

Magyarok Nagyasszonya Társaság

Szerb Antal u. 13-17
1021 Budapest
Tel: (1) 275-1395

Located near the pilgrimage sites of the Basilica of Saint Stephen and Our Lady of Remete.

Kalocsai Iskolanövérek

Mária u. 20
1085 Budapest
Tel: (1) 266-0519 • Fax: (1) 266-0528

Located near the pilgrimage sites of the Basilica of Saint Stephen and Our Lady of Remete.

Ferences Mária Misszionérius Növérek

Hermina u. 19
1146 Budapest
Tel: (1) 343-8003

Located near the pilgrimage sites of the Basilica of Saint Stephen and Our Lady of Remete.

Leanyfalu

Móriozzs ut. 141
Szent gellert Hàz
Tel: (26) 383-212 • Fax: (26) 383-302

Located near the pilgrimage sites of the Basilica of Saint Stephen and Our Lady of Remete.

Mater Salvatoris

Lelkigyakorlatos Ház
Kapucinusole tere 3
2100 Gödöllő-Máriabesnyő
Tel: (0628) 510-741, 510-742 • Tel/Fax: (0628) 420-176
Web Site: www.hotels.hu/mater_salvatoris

Located next to the shrine of Our Lady of Máriabesnyő.

Máriapócsi Kegytemplom

Kossuth Tér 25
4326 Máriapócs
Tel/Fax: (042) 385-528

Located adjacent to the famous Marian Hungarian shrine of Our Lady of Máriapócs, the Retreat Center and Pilgrim's House can accommodate up to one hundred and twenty people.

IRELAND

Knock House Hotel

Ballyhaunis Road
Knock, Co. Mayo
Tel: (094) 88-088 • Fax: (094) 88-044
E-mail: hotel@knock-shrine.ie
Web Site: www.knock-shrine.ie

Home to the shrine of Our Lady of Knock, the pilgrimage site where, in 1879, the Blessed Virgin Mary appeared to fifteen people.

Saint Patrick's Purgatory
Lough Derg
Pettigo, Co. Donegal
Tel/Fax: (072) 615-18
Web Site: www.loughderg.org

A place of pilgrimage dating back to the eighth century, it is the only one of a penitential nature remaining in the modern Christian world. One and three-day retreats are available.

ITALY

✠

Sisters of the Atonement
Via G. Alessi, 10
06081 Assisi (PG)
Tel: (075) 812-542 • Fax: (075) 813-723

Located near the world-famous shrine dedicated to Saint Francis of Assisi.

Sisters of Saint Bridget
Via Moiano, 1
06081 Assisi (PG)
Tel: (075) 812-693 • Fax: (075) 813-216

Located near the world-famous shrine dedicated to Saint Francis of Assisi.

Franciscan Missionary Sisters of Assisi
Via S. Francesco, 13
06081 Assisi
Tel: (075) 812-267 • Fax: (075) 816-258

Located near the world-famous shrine dedicated to Saint Francis of Assisi.

Domus Pacis

Basilica Patriarcale e Protoconventodella Porziuncola
Frazione di Santa Maria degli Angeli
06088 Assisi (PG)
Tel: (075) 80-40-455, (075) 80-511 • Fax: (075) 80-51-478

Located near the world-famous shrine dedicated to Saint Francis of Assisi.

Saint Anthony's Guest House

Via G. Alessi, 10
06081 Assisi (PG)
Tel: (075) 812-542 • Fax: (075) 813-723

Located near the world-famous shrine dedicated to Saint Francis of Assisi.

Monastero S. Colette

Borgo San Pietro, 3
06081 Assisi (PG)
Tel: (075) 812-345 • Fax: (075) 816-489

Located near the world-famous shrine dedicated to Saint Francis of Assisi.

Casa del Terziario

Piazza del Vescovado, 5
06081 Assisi (PG)
Tel: (075) 812-366 • Fax: (075) 816-377

Located near the world-famous shrine dedicated to Saint Francis of Assisi.

Hotel Ancajani

Via Ancanjani, 16
06081 Assisi (PG)
Tel: (075) 815-128 • Fax: (075) 815-129

Located near the world-famous shrine dedicated to Saint Francis of Assisi.

Casa Madonna Della Pace
Via Bernardo da Quintavalle, 16
06081 Assisi (PG)
Tel: (075) 812-337 • Fax: (075) 816-851

Located near the world-famous shrine dedicated to Saint Francis of Assisi.

Istituto Beata Angelina
Via Merry del Val, 4
06081 Assisi (PG)
Tel/Fax: (075) 812-511

Located near the world-famous shrine dedicated to Saint Francis of Assisi.

Benedettine S. Maria Del Monte
Corso Matteotti, 15
06031 Bevagna (PG)
Tel: (0742) 360-133
Web Site: www.benedettine.it

Provides a place of prayer, retreat, and warm hospitality.

Hotel Delle Rose
The House of the Pilgrim
Via Fasce, 2
06043 Cascia (PG)
Tel: (0743) 76-241 • Fax: (0743) 76-240
E-mail: hdr@netgen.it
Web Site: www.netgen.it/hdr

Located near the shrine and convent dedicated to Saint Rita of Cascia, where a eucharistic miracle dates back to 1330.

Abbazia di Maguzzano

Via Maguzzano, 6
25017 Lonato (BS)
Tel: (03) 913-01-82 • Fax: (03) 913-871
E-mail: abamaguz@tin.it

Provides more than fifty guest rooms for spiritual retreats.

Madonna di Loreto

Casa del Clero
Via Asdrubali, 104
60025 Loreto (AN)
Tel: (071) 97-02-98 • Fax: (071) 75-00-532

Located near the world-famous Holy House of Loreto, the site where the home of the Blessed Virgin Mary is said to have been carried by angels from the Holy Land to rest in the thirteenth century.

Sisters of the Holy Family of Nazareth

Via Maccari, 7
60025 Loreto (AN)
Tel: (071) 97-01-81 • Fax: (071) 75-04-604

Located near the world-famous Holy House of Loreto, the site where the home of the Blessed Virgin Mary is said to have been carried by angels from the Holy Land to rest in the thirteenth century.

Istituto Sacra Famiglia Piemonte

Via Asdrubali, 70
60025 Loreto (AN)
Tel/Fax: (071) 977-685

Located near the world-famous Holy House of Loreto, the site where the home of the Blessed Virgin Mary is said to have been carried by angels from the Holy Land to rest in the thirteenth century.

Orsoline Sisters
Via Montereale V, 96
60025 Loreto (AN)
Tel/Fax: (071) 97-01-92

Located near the world-famous Holy House of Loreto, the site where the home of the Blessed Virgin Mary is said to have been carried by angels from the Holy Land to rest in the thirteenth century.

Casa di Spiritualità
Via S. Salvadore, 54
50050 Malmantile (FI)
Tel: (055) 878-053 • Fax: (055) 872-9930

Provides a place of spiritual retreat for both men and women.

Convento Santuario di San Gerardo Majella
Piazzale Chiesa Nuova
83040 Materdomini (AV)
Tel: (0827) 58-486 • Fax: (0827) 58-498

Home to the shrine of Saint Gerard Majella.

Pilgrim's House
Piazza Carlo d'Angio
Monte Sant'Angelo
71037 Monte Sant'Angelo (FG)
Tel: (0884) 56-23-96 • Tel/Fax: (0884) 56-11-50
Web Site: www.gargano.it/sanmichele

Home to one of Christendom's most famous pilgrimage sites. Saint Michael the Archangel is said to have appeared at this place on several occasions in the fifth and seventeenth centuries.

Istituto "SS. Salvatore"

Dominican Missionary Sisters of S. Sisto
Via del Popolo, 1
05018 Orvieto
Tel/Fax: (0763) 34-29-10

Located near the Cathedral of Orvieto, which is home to a eucharistic miracle dating back to the thirteenth century. It is usually closed during the month of July.

Virgilio

Piazza Duomo, 5
05018 Orvieto
Tel: (0763) 34-18-82
Fax: (0763) 34-37-97

Located near the Cathedral of Orvieto, which is home to a eucharistic miracle dating back to the thirteenth century.

Pilgrim's House

Via M. Cesarotti, 21
35123 Padua
Tel: (049) 82-39-711 • Fax: (049) 82-39-780

Located adjacent to the shrine of Saint Anthony of Padua.

Abbazia di Santa Giustina

Via Giuseppe Ferrari, 2/A
35123 Padua (PD)
Tel: (049) 87-56-435 • Fax: (049) 66-60-02

Located adjacent to the shrine of Saint Anthony of Padua.

Our Lady of Atonement Guesthouse
Via Monte del Gallo, 105
00165 Rome
Tel: (06) 630-782 • Fax: (06) 638-6149
E-mail: atonerome@tiscalinet.it

Piccole Suore Della Sacra Famiglia
Casa di Accoglienza Paolo VI
Viale Vaticano, 92
00165 Rome
Fax: (06) 397-237-92
E-mail: casapaolovi@tiscalinet.it

Suore del Prez. Sangue di Monza
Via S. Maria Mediatrice, 8
00165 Rome
Tel: (06) 631-759

Instituto Madri Pie
Via Alcide de Gasperi, 4
00165 Rome
Tel: (06) 631-967, 633-441 • Fax: (06) 631-989

House of Our Lady of Fátima
Saint Dorothy Institude
Via del Gianicolo, 4/A
00165 Rome
Tel: (06) 688-03-349 • Fax: (06) 688-03-311

Villa Fátima
Oblates of the Most Holy Redeemer
Via Paolo Bentivoglio 1
00165 Rome
Tel/Fax: (06) 393-666-66

Sisters of Lourdes

Via Sistina 113
00187 Rome
Tel: (06) 474-5324 • Fax: (06) 474-1422

Casa del Pellegrino del Santuario

Via Ardeatina
00134 Rome
Tel: (06) 713-533-90, 713-533-92, 713-533-93 • Fax: (06) 713-533-94

Casa Santa Maria alle Fornaci

Piazza Santa Maria alle Fornaci, 27
00165 Rome
Tel: (06) 393-676-32 • Fax: (06) 393-667-95
E-mail: cffornaci@tin.it

Casa Kolbe

Via San Teodoro, 44
00186 Rome
Tel: (06) 679-49-74 • Fax: (06) 699-41-550

Alma Domus

Via di Camporegio 37
53100 Siena
Tel: (0577) 44-177 • Fax: (0577) 47-601

Located near the shrine dedicated to Saint Catherine of Siena.

Casa Ritiri S. Regina

Villa Santa Regina
Strada di S. Regina and Valdipugna
No. 6
53100 Siena
Tel: (0577) 22-12-06 • Fax: (0577) 282-329, 292-329

Located near the shrine dedicated to Saint Catherine of Siena.

POLAND

+‖+
+‖+

Auschwitz Center of Information & Dialogue

Centrum Dialogu I Modlitwy W Oświęcimiu
Ul. Maksymiliana Kolbego 1
32-602 Oświęcim
Tel: (033) 43-10-00 • Fax: (033) 43-10-01

The Center of Information, Meetings, Dialogue, Education, and Prayer (listed above) is owned and operated by the Catholic Church. Located one block from the Auschwitz camp, the center provides comfortable and quiet accommodations, a restaurant, helpful staff who speak English, French, and Polish, as well as a library and telephone/fax services.

Diecezjalny Dom Rekolekcyjny

SS. Sżarytki
Ul Sw Barbary 43
42-200 Częstochowa-Jasna Góra
Tel: (034) 324-11-77

Located near one of Eastern Europe's most famous Marian shrines, Our Lady of Częstochowa. A ten-minute walk from the sanctuary, this church-run hotel provides excellent accommodation for pilgrims.

SS. Brygidki (Sisters of Saint Brigid)

Ul. Elżbiety 11
42-225 Częstochowa
Tel: (034) 365-15-76

Located near one of Eastern Europe's most famous Marian shrines, Our Lady of Częstochowa.

SS. Franciszkanki (Franciscan Sisters)
Rodziny Maryi
Ul. Ks. Kard. Wyszyńskiego 77/79
42-225 Częstochowa
Tel: (034) 362-95-61

Located near one of Eastern Europe's most famous Marian shrines, Our Lady of Częstochowa.

Sanktuarium Maryjne w Gietrzwałdzie
11-036 Gietrzwałd
Tel: (089) 512-31-02, (089) 512-34-07 • Fax: (089) 512-34-06
E-mail: sanktuarium@at.pl

The Pilgrim's House is located adjacent to the shrine of Our Lady of Gietrzwald, the site of a Church-approved Marian apparition and a miraculous image of the Blessed Virgin Mary in northern Poland. To learn more about the shrine and apparitions, visit their Web site which provides information in English.

Dom Pielgrzyma im. bł.Jakuba Strzemię
Kalwaria Pacławska 40
37-743 Nowosiółki Dydyńskie
Tel: (016) 678-89-44

The Pilgrim's House, operated by the shrine of Kalwaria Pacławska, offers excellent accommodation.

Siostry Elzbietanki
Krzeszów Kamiennogorski 29
58-405 Krzeszów
Tel: (075) 74-123-35

Located near the pilgrimage shrine of Our Lady of Krzeszów.

Dom Pielgrzyma

11-407 Święta Lipka 29
Woj. Olsztyńskie
Tel: (089) 755-14-81 • Fax: (089) 755-14-60

The Pilgrim's House, operated by the pilgrimage sanctuary of Our Lady of Święta Lipka, offers very simple and basic accommodations.

Saint Hedwig of Silesia Pilgrim's House

Ul. Jana Pawla II 3
55–100 Trzebnica
Tel: (071) 312-11-18, (071) 312-14-15 • Fax: (071) 387-07-13

Located adjacent to the shrine of Saint Hedwig, the Pilgrim's House offers very comfortable accommodations.

PORTUGAL

Hotel Virgem Maria

Av. Dom José Alves Correia da Silva 40
2495 Fátima
Tel: (0249) 531-714, (0249) 532-777 • Fax: (0249) 532-703
E-mail: reserv@hotel-virgem-maria.com
Web Site: www.hotel-virgem-maria.com

Located near the world-famous shrine of Our Lady of Fátima, where, in 1917, the Blessed Virgin Mary appeared to three small children.

SPAIN

Hostal Hogar San Francisco

Campiño S. Francisco, 3
Santiago de Compostela
15-705 Coruña(Galicia)
Tel: (981) 572-463, 572-564
Fax: (981) 571-916

Located near the world-famous shrine of Santíago de Compostela.

Congregation of Our Lady of the Pillar

C/Castillo de Javier, 514 s/n
Apdo. 4097
50013 Zaragoza
Tel: (976) 41-61-85

Located near the shrine of Our Lady of Zaragoza, where, in the first century, the Blessed Virgin Mary appeared to Saint James the Apostle.

House of the Spiritual Exercises

"Quinta Julieta"
Paseo del Canal s/n, 144
50007 Zaragoza
Tel: (976) 27-21-50

Located near the shrine of Our Lady of Zaragoza, where, in the first century, the Blessed Virgin Mary appeared to Saint James the Apostle.

Part 5

⳨

Other European Monasteries & Convents

EVEN THOUGH many of the following monasteries and convents do not currently provide guesthousing, most of them are worth a visit on either a day trip or for a retreat. It is for this reason I have included them, and provided their contact information. Each of them can be accessed via the Internet.

AUSTRIA

Benediktinerstift Admont

Kulturessort
8911 Admont
Tel: (3613) 2312-601 • Fax: (3613) 2312-46, (3613) 2312-610
E-mail: kultur@stiftadmont.at
Web Site: www.stiftadmont.at

Benediktinerabtei Altenburg

Abt Placidus Much-Straße 1
A-3591 Altenburg, NÖ
Tel: (02982) 3451-21 • Fax: (02982) 3451-13
E-mail: kultur.tourismus@stift-altenburg.at
Web Site: www.stift-altenburg.at

Augustiner–Chorherrenstift Herzogenburg

A-3130 Herzogenburg
Tel: (02782) 83112-0 • Fax: (02782) 83113
E-mail: stift@herzogenburg.at
Web Site: www.herzogenburg.at/stift

Stift Klosterneuburg

Stiftsplatz 1
3400 Klosterneuburg
Tel: (02243) 411-0 • Fax: (02243) 411-156
E-mail: kultur@stift-klosterneuburg.at
Web Site: www.stift-klosterneuburg.at

Stift Kremsmünster

4550 Kremsmünster
Tel: (07583) 275-0, (07583) 275-216 • Fax: (07583) 275-288
Web Site: www.stift-kremsmuenster.at

Stift Lilienfeld

Klosterrotte 1
3180 Lilienfeld
Tel: (2762) 524-20, 524-20-0, 522-04 • Fax: (2762) 522-924
Web Site: www.stift-lilienfeld.at

ENGLAND

Saint Hugh's Charterhouse

Partridge Green
Horsham, West Sussex RH13 8EB
Tel: (1403) 864-231 • Fax: (1403) 864-758
Web Site: www.parkminster.org.uk

Tyburn Convent

8, Hyde Park Place
London W2 2LJ
Fax: (171) 706-4507
E-mail: mg@tyburnconvent.org.uk
Web Site: www.tyburnconvent.org.uk

Glastonbury Abbey (Anglican Church)

The Abbey Gatehouse
Magdalene Street
Glastonbury, Somerset BA6 9EL
Tel/Fax: (1458) 832-267
E-mail: glastonbury.abbey@dial.pipex.com
Web Site: www.glastonburyabbey.com

FRANCE

Monastère de la Grande Chartreuse
38380 Saint-Pierre-de-Chartreuse
Tel (Abbey): (04) 76-88-60-30, 76-88-62-17 • Fax: (04) 76-88-61-08
Web Site: http://www.chartreux.org

Founded in 1084, the famous Monastery of La Grande Chartreuse is home to a community of Carthusian monks. This is the charterhouse where Saint Bruno first founded the Carthusian Order—hence its world-renowned fame and importance within the Catholic Church. Due to the seclusion of the Carthusian monks, you cannot visit the entire hermitage, but you can learn more about them via their Web site.

GERMANY

Benediktinerabtei Gerleve
Abtei Saint Joseph
48727 Billerbeck
Tel: (2541) 800-0
Fax: (2541) 800-203, (2541) 800-233
Web Site: www.benediktiner-orden.de/users/gerleve

Kloster Andechs
Bergstrasse 2
82346 Andechs
Tel: (8152) 37-60
Fax: (8152) 37-62-60
Web Site: www.andechs.de

Abtei Saint Stephan

Stephansplatz 6
86152 Augsburg
Tel: (821) 32-960 • Fax: (821) 32-961-23
E-mail: abtei@st-stephan.de
Web Site: www.st-stephan.de

Erzabtei Saint Martin

88631 Beuron
Tel: (7466) 17-0 • Fax: (7466) 17-107
E-mail: verwaltung@erzabtei-beuron.de
Web Site: www.erzabtei-beuron.de

Kloster Helfta

Monika Sattler
Lindenstrasse 36
06295 Lutherstadt Eisleben
Tel: (3475) 71-54-50 • Fax: (3475) 71-54-52
Web Site: www.kloster-helfta.de

Benediktinerabtei Königsmünster

Postfach 1161
59851 Meschede
Tel: (291) 299-50 • Fax: (291) 299-51-00
E-mail: abtei@koenigsmuenster.de
Web Site: www.koenigsmuenster.de

Benediktinerabtei

Abteistr. 3
94526 Metten
Tel: (991) 9108-0 • Fax: (991) 9108-211, (991) 9108-100
E-mail: Benediktinerstift-Metten@t-online.de
Web Site: www.kloster-metten.de

Benediktinerinnenabtei Saint Hildegard
Postfach 1320
65378 Rüdesheim am Rhein
Tel: (6722) 499-0 • Fax: (6722) 499-185
Web Site: www.abtei-st-hildegard.de

Erzabtei Saint Ottilien
86941 Saint Ottilien
Tel: (8193) 710, (8193) 712-61 • Fax: (8193) 713-32, (8193) 6844
Web Site: www.erzabtei.de

Benediktinerabtei Saint Mauritius
Postfach 1060
66636 Tholey/Saar
Tel: (6853) 91-04-0 • Fax: (6853) 302-23
Web Site: www.hasler.net/abtei.htm

Abtei Schweiklberg
Postfach 240
94471 Vilshofen
Tel: (8541) 209-0 • Fax: (8541) 209-174, (8541) 209-219
E-mail: bruder_berthold@vilstal.net
Web Site: www.schweiklberg.de

Benediktinerkloster
Markt 12
09306 Wechselburg
Tel: (37384) 808-11 • Fax: (37384) 808-33, (37384) 808-22
E-mail: verwaltung@kloster-ettal.de
Web Site: www.kloster-ettal.de/wechselburg

HUNGARY

Archabbey of Pannonhalma

9090 Pannonhalma, Var 1
Tel: (36) (96) 470-022 • Fax: (36) (96) 470-011
Web Site: www.osb.hu/english

Tihany Abbey

Batthyany u. 34
8238 Tihany
Tel: (36) (86) 348-405 • Fax: (36) (86) 348-068

ITALY

Monastero SS. Salvatore

Benedettine dell'Adorazione del SS. Sacramento
Via Stazione 1
22070 Grandate (Como)
Tel: (031) 564-823
Web Site: www.cometacom.it/monastero/grandate/home.htm

Monastero Trappiste Nostra Signora di San Giuseppe

Via della Stazione, 19
01030 Vitorchiano (Viterbo)
Tel: (0761) 37-00-17 • Fax: (0761) 37-09-52
E-mail: vitorchiano@iol.it
Web Site: www.vitorchiano.org

SPAIN

Abadia N.Sra de la Oliva

31310 Carcastillo (Navarra)
Tel: (948) 72-50-06 • Fax: (948) 71-50-55
E-mail: ocsolaoliva@planalfa.es
Web Site: www.navarnet.com/laoliva

SWITZERLAND

Zisterzienserinnen-Abtei

Mariazell-Wurmsbach
8715 Bollingen (SG)
Tel: (055) 212-32-32 • Fax: (055) 212-72-89
E-mail: wurmsbach@kath.ch
Web Site: http://www.kath.ch/wurmsbach

Abbaye Saint-Benoît-de-Port-Valais

Rte de l'Eglise 38
1897 Le Bouveret (VS)
Tel: (24) 4-812-812 • Fax: (24) 4-814-398
Web Site: www.abbaye-saint-benoit.ch

Abtei Saint Otmarsberg

Ernetschwilerstrasse
Postfach 135
8730 Uznach
Tel: (55) 280-71-61, 71-11-61 • Fax: (55) 290-13-74, 72-26-23
E-mail: st.otmarsberg@abtei-uznach.ch
Web Site: www.abtei-uznach.ch

Part 6

Appendices

Monastic-Related Web Sites

AUSTRIAN ABBEYS
  http://www.noe.co.at/kloesterreich

AUGUSTINIAN ORDER
  http://www.aug.org

BENEDICTINE ORDER
  http://www.osb.org

BENEDICTINE ORDER (SUBIACO CONGREGATION)
  http://www.subiaco.nm.org

CAMALDOLESE ORDER
  http://www.contemplation.com

CARMELITE ORDER
  http://www.ocarm.org

CARTHUSIAN ORDER
  http://www.chartreux.org

CISTERCIAN ORDER OF THE STRICT OBSERVANCE (TRAPPISTS)
  http://www.ocso.org

CISTERCIAN ORDER OF THE STRICT OBSERVANCE (TRAPPISTS)—USA
  http://www.cistercian-usa.org

CISTERCIAN PUBLICATIONS
  http://www.spencerabbey.org/cistpub

CLUNY (HISTORIC BENEDICTINE MONASTERY)
  www.uni-muenster.de/Fruehmittelalter/Projekte/Cluny/links_cluny.htm

DISCALCED CARMELITE ORDER
  http://www.ocd.pcn.net/index_en.htm

DOMINICAN ORDER
http://www.op.org

ENGLISH BENEDICTINE CONGREGATION
http://www.benedictines.org.uk/

FRANCISCAN ORDER
http://www.ofm.org

FRANCISCAN ORDER, CAPUCHINS
http://www.capuchins.org

FRANCISCAN ORDER, CONVENTUAL
http://www.ofmconv.org

FRENCH MONASTERIES
http://www.abbayes.net

GREGORIAN CHANT RESOURCES
http://www.solesmes.com
http://comp.uark.edu/~rlee/otherchant.html

LINKS TO CATHOLIC RESOURCES
http://www.newadvent.org

LINKS TO MONASTIC RESOURCES
http://www.newadvent.org

LINKS TO MONASTIC SITES
http://www.geocities.com/~catolicos/monaster.htm

LINKS TO RELIGIOUS ORDERS
http://www.catholic-forum.com/links/pages/Religious_Orders

MONASTERIES & RELIGIOUS COMMUNITIES IN SWITZERLAND
http://www.kath.ch/orden-ordres

NEW CATHOLIC ENCYCLOPEDIA
An excellent resource for further study:
http://www.newadvent.org/cathen

TRAPPIST BEER WEB SITES
http://www.chimay.be
http://www.orval.be
http://www.trappistwestmalle.be
http://www.latrappe.nl

VATICAN WEB SITE & RESOURCES
http://www.vatican.va
http://www.christusrex.org

VOCATIONS WEB SITE
http://www.religiouslife.com

Note: By visiting these home pages, you will find excellent links to other monastic-related Web sites.

SPECIAL NOTE

To view maps representing the locations of the monasteries and convents, you can visit the Web site www.catholicadventures.com.

INTERNET TRAVEL RESOURCES & WEB SITES

CATHOLIC TRAVEL GUIDEBOOKS

This site provides information about Kevin J. Wright's award-winning books *Catholic Shrines of Western Europe: A Pilgrim's Travel Guide* and *Catholic Shrines of Central & Eastern Europe: A Pilgrim's Travel Guide.*

http://www.catholicadventures.com/guidebooks.html

CATHOLIC INTERNET PORTAL

Provides Internet users a unique experience in which their Christian faith and life can intersect.

http://www.catholicexchange.com

CATHOLIC PILGRIMAGE INFORMATION

http://www.catholicpilgrims.com

CATHOLIC TRAVEL PRODUCTS & RESOURCES

http://www.pilgrimageshop.com

CIA WORLD FACTBOOK

http://www.odci.gov/cia/publications/factbook/index.html

CURRENCY CONVERSIONS

http://www.xe.net/ucc
http://www.oanda.com/cgi-bin/travel

E-MAIL

If you plan to use the Internet while traveling abroad, it is important to obtain an e-mail account which can be accessed from anywhere in the world. The following Internet portal provides web-based free e-mail service:

http://www.catholicexchange.com

EUROPEAN NATIONAL TOURIST OFFICES

Austria	http://www.austria-tourism.at
Belgium	http://www.visitbelgium.com
Britain	http://www.visitbritain.com
Croatia	http://www.htz.hr
Czech Republic	http://www.czech.cz

Denmark	http://www.dt.dk
France	http://www.franceguide.com
Germany	http://www.germany-tourism.de
Greece	http://www.greek-tourism.gr
Holland	http://www.goholland.com
Hungary	http://www.gotohungary.com
Ireland	http://www.ireland.travel.ie
Italy	http://www.italiantourism.com
Luxembourg	http://www.visitluxembourg.com
Norway	http://www.norway.org
Poland	http://www.polandtour.org
Portugal	http://www.portugal.org
Spain	http://www.okspain.org
Switzerland	http://www.switzerlandtourism.com
Turkey	http://www.turkey.com

EUROPEAN TRAVEL COMMISSION
http://www.visiteurope.com

HEALTH & TRAVEL INFORMATION
Provides health information, country descriptions, entry requirements, and embassy and consulate locations:

http://www.tripprep.com
http://travel.state.gov

HOTELS
Provides a listing of more than 50,000 hotels:

http://www.hotelguide.ch

Provides an index of more than 10,000 hotel sites around the world, organized geographically:

http://www.all-hotels.com

Provides a list of hostels:

http://www.hostels.com

Lodging Guide Worldwide:

http://www.lgww.com

INTERNET CAFÉ LISTINGS
Internet Cafés are coffee shops with computers which give travelers access to the Internet. The cost is typically approximately $5 for each half-hour. Internet Cafés provide one of the most useful and exciting ways to keep in

touch with family and friends while traveling abroad. These "modern-day" coffee-shops can be found in most major European cities, including Kraków (Poland), Budapest (Hungary), Vienna (Austria), Athens (Greece), and Prague (Czech Republic). For a full listing of the location of these cafés, visit these sites:

> http://www.netcafes.com/
> http://www.netcafeguide.com

Searching the Internet for Information About Monasteries or Catholic Shrines & Places of Pilgrimage

When searching the Internet to obtain information about monasteries or Catholic shrines and places of pilgrimage, there are a few important keywords to use: "Monasteries," "European Abbeys," "Trappist," "Cistercian," "Benedictine," "Catholic Shrines," "Catholic Shrines of Europe," "Catholic Pilgrimage," "Catholic Pilgrimage Tours," "Catholic Travel," "Catholic Tourism," and "Marian Shrines."

Tourism Bureaus and Embassies

Provides addresses and phone numbers for tourism offices around the globe:

> http://www.towd.com

Provides embassy information and links:

> http://www.embpage.org

Travel Accessories & Rail Passes

Provides travel accessories, guidebooks, rail passes & information:

> http://www.ricksteves.com

Train Information

Provides information and the sale of European passes:

> http://www.ricksteves.com/services/railmenu.htm

Provides information and the sale of Eurail passes:

> http://www.eurail.com
> http://www.raileurope.com

Provides fares and timetables for the 1,500 most traveled routes in Europe:

> http://www.raileurope.com

TRAVEL INFORMATION ABROAD

U.S. Department of State's Travel Warnings & Consular
Information Sheets:
   http://travel.state.gov/travel_warnings.html
Visa Requirements:
   http://travel.state.gov/foreignentryreqs.html

TRAVEL INFORMATION & NOTES

http://www.travelnotes.org

WORLDWIDE WEATHER FORECASTS

http://www.weather.com
http://www.intellicast.com

INDEX

ABOUT THE AUTHOR

KEVIN J. WRIGHT is the founder and president of Catholic Adventures International (www.catholicadventures.com), a provider of pilgrimage, adventure, and cruise trips to Europe, North America, the Caribbean, and beyond. In 1995, Kevin introduced the concept of "travel guidebooks" into the Catholic publishing industry and is today the author of the award-winning books *Catholic Shrines of Western Europe: A Pilgrim's Travel Guide, Catholic Shrines of Central & Eastern Europe: A Pilgrim's Travel Guide,* and *Europe's Monastery and Convent Guesthouses: A Pilgrim's Travel Guide.* He has backpacked through eighteen European countries and visited more than one hundred fifty places of pilgrimage. He has led guided tours to Europe and the Holy Land, served as a contributing writer to the National Catholic Register, and appeared on several national radio and television programs, including EWTN's *Life on the Rock* and *Onward Pilgrims.* With his newest book *Living Your Life With Purpose and Passion: A Catholic Vision,* Kevin has once again broke new ground within the publishing industry by introducing the concept of "Catholic personal development and leadership books." To learn more about this publication or to sign up for his monthly *Purpose & Passion* e-mail newsletter, you can visit his Web site at www.purposeandpassion.com. You will also find information here about his *Living Your Life With Purpose and Passion* products, materials, retreats, trips, and workshops, as well as information on hiring Kevin as a motivational speaker or consultant for your school, organization, business, or conference.